W9-AIB-514

The Deer Pasture

The Deer Pasture

by RICK BASS

Drawings by ELIZABETH HUGHES BASS

W·W·NORTON & COMPANY
NEW YORK   LONDON

HOWARD COUNTY LIBRARY
BIG SPRING, TEXAS

Copyright © 1985 by Rick Bass
All rights reserved

Library of Congress Cataloging in Publication Data

Bass, Rick, 1958–
The deer pasture.

1. Deer hunting—Texas—Gillespie County.   I. Title.
II. Series.
SK301.B358   1985   976.4'65   84-16292
ISBN 0-393-31435-9

First published as a Norton paperback 1989
by arrangement with Texas A & M University Press; reissued 1996

W. W. Norton & Company, Inc., 500 Fifth Avenue, New York, N.Y. 10110
W. W. Norton & Company Ltd., 10 Coptic Street, London WC1A 1PU

Manufactured in the United States of America

2 3 4 5 6 7 8 9 0

For Old Timer and Old Charlie
and, of course,
Grandaddy

Contents

Preface

THE place I'm going to write about, the deer pasture—I don't live there. I wish I did, but I have to make a living. I went to work in Mississippi, where there isn't any granite, and where there aren't any ringtails. These people were the first to offer me a job; they were the only people to offer me a job. It's sort of an administrative job, with, well, I'm sort of ashamed to admit it, but with a desk, and a big phone, one of those kinds you have to push a flashing yellow light on to talk, and there's even a secretary. There's a typewriter too, and lots of bookshelves.

There are no windows. In one corner of my office there is one of those postcard calendars with a different picture each month: Pedernales Falls, White-Tail Family, Young Raccoons—under each picture there are little titles designed to make me incredibly homesick for Gillespie County and the deer pasture.

I was the only one of my friends to get a job. Most of them went on to graduate school. One of them opened a car wash. Ken went back up to Wyoming to trap beaver and sell furs and fish through the ice in winter. He started growing a beard even before he graduated and spent his last few weeks sewing buckskin leggings and shirts so that by the time he took his last final, he was all ready to go. He wore his buckskins to class, sat on the front row, took the final (Advanced Seminar in Genetics), finished it, laid it on the desk, then ran out of the classroom without making a sound. No whoop, no smile, no nothing—he just turned and ran. He was wearing his moccasins; he was as silent as a quick thought as he ran. It was eerie. We heard his truck start up; we heard him drive away in a hurry.

When I signed on for this job in Mississippi, it startled my friends, puzzled my professors. My parents breathed a sigh of relief that could be heard 'round the world. My younger brothers snickered and made secret bets with each other on whether I'd quit on an odd month or an even one, on whether I'd quit before my first paycheck, and on whether I'd even unpack before deciding I didn't like Jackson.

Too close to New Orleans, they said.

Not close enough to the deer pasture, thought I.

Sometimes, I have to wear a coat and tie. I had to learn to iron. Also, it became necessary to do this: to figure out which fork to eat salad with.

When I left school for Jackson, I was able to stuff everything I owned in the back of my little Rabbit. It was a sad feeling, very frightening, actually, leaving the security of the mountains, traveling downhill like that, out of the crispness of the high country and into the hot torpor of the flatlands, but it was also a good feeling, being able to contain myself and all my possessions in one small orange car that would go forty-two miles on a gallon of gas. I believe I even hummed a little as I drove.

Whistling in the dark.

When I got to Jackson, I was glad I had brought the little cedar tree. It was a pretty one, and until I found a tiny one-room cell of an efficiency apartment to stay in, it so completely filled my hotel room with the sappy, sprightly clean smell of the deer pasture that upon awakening in the morning, for the first few seconds I would forget where I was. Or rather, where I wasn't.

In my new cubicle of an apartment, however, there wasn't room for both the tree and the canoe, so one night by the dark of the moon I planted it in the center of the

City Hall flower garden, right beneath the statue of Andrew Jackson. I wore black jeans and a black sweater and camouflage make-up; I ran low and crouched over, and dug the hole with a little hand shovel. When I was through, I tamped the soil down and watered it.

On coffee breaks, I can step outside my building and see the cedar. So far, it's doing fine; it's holding its own. Whenever possible, I take my lunch break over there and eat deviled eggs and tunafish sandwiches in front of it and close my eyes and take deep, satisfied breaths; it smells so good.

On rainy days I bring an umbrella. I fertilize the little tree regularly, and when no one else is around, I sometimes sing to it. They say that helps plants—that it makes them grow better.

This one's started dropping a few needles, but I'm not too concerned . . . not yet. The soil is right—I checked it out—and the temperature's okay, as are the water requirements. I mean, technically, everything the tree needs to stay alive is there.

So why is it losing needles?

In my desk, at work, this is what I keep rolled up in the bottom drawer: a road map of Gillespie County and the Texas Hill Country.

The Deer Pasture

I
The Deer Pasture

THESE are the names of the places I hunt: Buck Hill, the Water Gap, the Burned-Off Hill, Camp Creek, the East Side, the Back Side of Buck Hill, and Turkey Hollow.

In the old days, the big ravine, Turkey Hollow, used to be called Panther Holler and then Black Bear Holler and then just "the Holler." You see a lot of coons down there now, even in the daytime. It's dark and shady, and has near-vertical bluffs. In the fall the hickories turn gold and drop a ton of leaves down into the creek. The water in the creek is clear and cold and still; ocher hickory leaves stare back at you from the bottom when you bend over the creek, and you can see your reflection. It's about two miles from the camphouse, but it takes you over an hour to get there. It's an oasis, a place to come to, a surprise; you don't get many hardwood-hickory creek bottoms in the Hill Country of Texas.

It's near Willow City and Stonewall, where we hunt, which is near Eckert, which is near Llano. When you come into Llano, there is a sign that tells you you are entering the deer hunting capital of the world. When we are in need of a jeep part, or flour, or to make a phone call, we go into Fredericksburg. People are friendly in Fredericksburg. They're friendly in Willow City and Stonewall and Eckert and Llano, too.

The lease is nine hundred and fifty-six acres, only we don't call it the lease; that's too impersonal, too businesslike. We call it the deer pasture. We, the Basses, have

been hunting it for forty-nine years now; my grandfather is the only one who's made all forty-nine trips. Uncle Jimmy's next, with forty-seven, and my father, Charlie, has forty-five. Cousin Randy and I have three trips under our belts; this year will be our fourth. We're in love with the place as much as our fathers are, maybe even more so, which is like a present to them, since they used to worry about that. The other men in the family, younger and older cousins and brothers, they like it all right, but they aren't as consumed by it.

Uncle Jimmy and Pop are glad to see us so crazy about the deer pasture. They know now that as long as we're around, it's good for another forty-nine years of Bass hunters. At least. They'll be gone then, surely, but that'll make ninety-eight years. Cousin Randy and I are already making plans for the one hundredth anniversary. Randy'll be eighty. I'll be seventy-seven.

In 1937, the third year they'd been hunting there, Grandaddy (with black hair—I have pictures to prove it) and Uncle Jimmy (pudgy, baby-faced) saw a white buck run through the meadow below the Old Moss Tree. An albino. A twelve-point. Chasing does.

Grandaddy fired, missed.

For the one hundredth anniversary, what we intend to do is buy a bunch of black bears, all sizes and ages, males and females, maybe a hundred or so, and turn them loose in the Hill Country. In Turkey Hollow. We'll run banging

pans at them, shouting at them in their startled freedom, and chase them off into the caves and creeks and canyons and draws, the way it used to be, before they all got shot up.

Unlike the grizzlies, black bears didn't run out of habitat. They ran out of bears. The habitat is still there. The country is still perfect for bears. Cousin Randy and I are convinced of this.

Our sons and daughters will hike the deer pasture and see the bear tracks in the sand washes, see their fur on trees, smell their musty sign in caves and under big ledges, hear talk in the post office of how someone shot one a couple years ago, and see one every now and then, in a meadow early in the morning, far from any roads, just a movement disappearing into the cedars, and they'll be excited. . . .

If any one sees us releasing the bears and wonders what all those bears are doing scrambling across rock ledges and loping across granite ridges, we'll tell them this: they escaped. We're going to transport them in the back of a big eighteen-wheel tractor-trailer with straw spread down all over the floor. With luck we will not be questioned about what two old geezers were doing with one hundred black bears in the first place. There are little logistical things to be worked out, trifling details that over the years must be ironed out for the plan to work properly, but they are small and insignificant and the years many. For instance, neither of us has a commercial trucker's license; neither one of us knows how to drive a semi.

These things can be worked out.

There are lots of deer on the deer pasture—lots more than there used to be. On Camp Creek two years ago, coming back in to lunch, working our way through boulders as big as Volkswagens, boulders as big as small towns, even, Cousin Randy and I jumped up six deer—five does and a spike.

These are, I suppose, the good old days.

I know that a lot of you are aware that Texas has more white-tailed deer—*Odocoileus virginianus*, write the scientists in papers presented at game management seminars—than any other region in the world and that of this Texas deer-hunting phenomenon, the heart, the focal point, the hot-spot, the center of all this activity, is the Hill Country: north of San Antonio, west of Austin, out across Lampasas, west of what geologists and other students of the earth call the Balcones Escarpment. It's a severely twisted and faulted region of cactus and rattlesnakes and canyons and hills that spring up out of the Gulf Coastal Plains like serrated ridges on a dinosaur's back—stegosaurus, ankylosaurus, that sort of company.

So it's a tough area, famed for having lots of deer. There are probably a few people, however, who do not know just how many. In 1983, Texans harvested over 16,000 tons of white-tailed deer, and that wasn't even close to its 1975 record of 17,500 tons. Half a million hunters

spent well over three hundred million dollars—some esti-
mates run as high as half a billion—in their pursuit of the
nation's number one big game animal. According to the
Texas Parks and Wildlife Department, there are three million deer in the state—about one on every twenty-two
acres. And in some deer-rich areas, such as Gillespie
County and the Johnson City area, densities may reach the
unhealthful level of one deer per six acres. Six acres is not a
very big space for an animal like a deer to live on.

Also in 1983, Texas deer hunters spent a combined
total of 3,482,226 days in the field hunting white-tails.

In 1935, the year the Basses started hunting the deer
pasture, there were only 232,000 deer in the entire state—
one-fourteenth of the present population. Those deer
were, of course, bigger; their horns, hanging in the back of
the garage, more bleached and ancient than the recent
ones, are enormous.

So there are more deer; these are the good old days. They are everywhere. While walking through the woods, through sloping stands of post oaks browsed up to just below your eye level, or hiking the creek bottoms, or moving through the cedars—especially moving through the cedars—you can jump them up like quail; their white flags bound and zag up the sides of hills, their hooves clatter against stone. There are too many deer in the Hill Country and always have been since the bears and panthers went away. The first-year deer are about the size of big goats. Bucks with spike antlers are common (whether through poor nutrition or poor genes or both, no one can agree), and usually the only big does are the barren ones who have spent all summer eating instead of nursing a fawn along.

This is not to say that there are no big deer left in the Hill Country; there are still deer of tremendous proportions—wise three-, four-, and five-year-old bucks, typical and atypical, with thick necks and spreading rocking-chair horns that get tangled in the brush and make clacking noises as they move through the trees. Bucks that lie down on their belly when they hear a hunter and do not run but lie still and hide and wait until he is gone before silently sneaking off and away from that area for good, forever. Bucks that feed only at night, and sleep in the day, and have no friends, no other deer they travel with, for fear one of the other deer will do something stupid that will affect all of them—step on a twig, twitch a tail, snort a blow, step into a pasture at the wrong time. Instead, they drift through the woods alone, browsing acorns, growing fat, getting older, raising their heads and staring down the creek bottoms whenever they hear any sound at all, even a natural one.

You see a picture of one of these deer every now and then in the newspaper, on the front page of the *Bandera Bulletin*, the *Marble Falls Highlander*, the *Fredericksburg*

Standard, the *Boerne Star.* The hunters who bag them are nearly always grinning. Each year I tell myself that if I see such a deer, I will pass him up, just sit silently and watch him, and leave him to help generate yet another generation of thick-necked Hill Country monsters, but each year, when I hear hooves clattering faintly against rock, and see the tawn flash through the cedars, I do this: I raise my scope, and listen to the heavy sound of my heart, and wait breathless. My heart beats.

2
Rabbits and Hawks

HOWARD'S eighty-three. He's the rancher we lease the deer pasture from, one year at a time, year by year. He runs too many cattle on his place in Gillespie County. They're all Herefords. They stare at you with heavy ankles and bulging eyes when you come upon them in the woods, stare at you for several seconds with bovine indecision before waiting until the last instant, at which point they become convinced that you are coming after them with intent to butcher, and with wild alarm they will clamber up the rocky hills or charge off into the cedars with startling speed and agility as well as a disturbing amount of noise. The calves are the worst. With unerring stupidity they run in straight lines, straight through the area you had intended to hunt. They run a ways, stop, and look back; if you are still coming, if you are walking on a vector within even ninety degrees towards them, they'll snort and take off again—they are so stupid. They infuriate Grandaddy.

Cousin Randy and I are less intense, not self-assured enough to be disturbed by all the cattle. We've only been hunting the deer pasture a few years. We walk around exploring its wild beauty as if still afraid it may suddenly be whisked away from us. We don't have the gall yet to think angry thoughts about it, not about any of it. It's all too beautiful; we're still too new. Nothing bothers us. We think it's beautiful even when it rains.

Especially when it rains.

We don't tell Grandaddy these things. He doesn't like

the rain, because in November it nearly always turns to snow, and becomes generally and all-around hellishly cold and miserable and uncomfortable for an eighty-four-year-old man, and the wind blows, and the branches clack ice-laden against the tin roof at night, and everyone in Gillespie County, Texas, knows you can't hunt deer in the snow.

The biggest deer we ever shot on the place was in the snow in 1973.

Hunting the third week in November as we do, year in and year out, you can notice things that would not be noticed on a less-controlled and more random series of visits, such as February one year and September the next.

Some Novembers you can see rabbits everywhere. We've learned through experience that this means for the next couple of Novembers, in the evenings, we will be able to hear lots of coyotes on the place. If we see lots of coyotes and foxes, as we did this year, we'll know that we'll have a couple of years of reprieve before the rabbits return.

I used to think coyotes and foxes were anathema to cows and calves; I used to entertain thoughts that this is what the cattle had nightmares about: glowing red eyes in the moonlight, the musty scent of vixen in the wind, and the cry of coyotes under a full moon. After hunting last year, I now know that this is not so.

What they really fear is the rabbits.

The index, the key to all the barometers that Randy and I use to tell what next November will be like, is the grass. There's not much in Gillespie County—it's mostly all rock canyons and granite ledges and cedar and scrub oak, with lots of slickrock up on the tops of the mountains—but there are a few meadows, enough to make it nice, enough to make it beautiful.

Hawks wheel overhead, their thin, fierce, shrieking kee-kees carrying all over the mountain. The grass is low, for there are too many rabbits. The hawks dive out of the sky and snatch them up; the grass grows back. Next November, the hawks are gone. The rabbits return. The grass grows short again. The cattle low at night and move into the woods and strip leaves and browse from the trees, from the bark, even. The deer leave. The coyotes move in, and the foxes come out of the rocks, and they chase the rabbits. They catch them and kill them, eat them and feed them to their kits and pups, and the grass grows again, and the red rust coats of the cattle are pretty in the sunshine. The meadows are lush and green, and the rabbits begin to grow in number. The cattle sigh, and it starts all over again, but the cattle do the best they can. They know how to handle these things; have you ever noticed how you never see twin birthings of calves anymore in Gillespie County?

The rabbits freeze when the hawk passes over; they quiver when they hear the yap of the fox, the bark of the coyote. The grass grows back again.

Except what sometimes happens is this:

Have you ever seen a cow's tooth? It's not long and fangy, not like a wolf's; it is square and blocky and doesn't look at all dangerous. It's not something you look at and picture blood dripping from the way you do a real tooth, such as you will find on a coyote or a dog.

Cows don't slaver; cows don't bite the mailman. What they do instead, if it means keeping their young alive and

keeping themselves alive, is eat the grass down to the dirt. To the quick, to the roots, to the slow death from which there is no recovery. Hawks and coyotes, foxes and owls can only do so much.

Grandaddy shoots hawks, illegal, of course, when he sees them, hangs the hides of coyotes on the side of the bunkhouse, and makes old mountain-man shawls out of the foxes. Randy and I freeze when we see hawks and owls gliding through the woods on a silent stalk; we hold tight and watch them hunt and pray that they will be successful.

It's a balancing act: people, calves, owls, grass, and rabbits. Deer and foxes, coyotes and hawks. Cousin Randy and I try to keep an eye on things, notice them from year to year.

For a place we visit only one week out of the year, we worry about it far too much.

3
Hunter's Moon

I guess I ought to tell you about the moon in Gillespie County; it's just that I don't know where to start. It is a hunter's moon. This is not to be confused with a moon you hunt under. A hunter's moon speaks of hunts and chases to come. It is most potent when you are farthest away from an actual hunt. Bluegill season and dog days. Summertime. The secret of a hunter's moon is that it makes you remember things.

A description would be the logical place to begin telling you of the Gillespie County hunter's moon, except I wouldn't be able to do a very good job, because all the while I was describing it, I would be thinking ahead to how I was going to tell you all the things this moon does to you.

If you are lucky, that is.

And anyway, it changes; it's orange in the early light, right as it clears the trees—really sort of scary looking, if you ask me—it's so close it seems it's going to reach out and grab you—and then when it clears the last mountain, it's grown butter yellow, and by the time you go to sleep, if you are in the habit of going to sleep at midnight, it is as white as a bleached skull.

I really don't know of a better moon in the whole country to chase coons under. It drives the dogs crazy. Buck and Oso, Howard's hounds, know beyond a shadow of a doubt that they are the luckiest hounds on earth to be able to live on Howard's farm up north of Johnson City and have that old moon come up every night. You know they are thinking this; you can see it in the way they grin and loll their tongues and sleep in the dust in the daytime during September, when the days and nights start to grow crisp.

Waiting for dusk, they are.

Uncle Jimmy says the Hill Country moon makes you crazy if it shines on you too much, or if you sleep under it all night long too many times.

Howard sleeps with his windows open, even in winter. He goes to bed around nine every night. He can look out the old stone window and see the moon; he can see it light up his bedroom like a floodlight when it's full. He's been doing that since he was a young man.

We should all be so crazy.

I guess whatever it is bad that that old Gillespie County moon does to you, Cousin Randy and I have already got it. In fact, I'd go as far as to say we're eaten up with it. Terminal cases, we are.

Howard's been talking about having a new rock house on the place for about thirty years now.

Last July, we told him we'd help him build one. To replace the big old rock castle of a house he was living in. The one he'd always lived in.

We told him we'd lift the rocks and hand-tote the water from the creek to mix with the mud and gravel chat to make mortar cement. We told him we'd hew cedars.

Understand, we're talking July. Rattlesnakes and dragonflies. No wind. No wildlife out. Even the shade is hot.

Sometimes at the deer pasture up in the boulders, looking down a canyon shirtless and exposed up on the bare pink granite slickrock under the hot butter yellow sun, you imagine you hear a steady buzzing, but of course that is ridiculous, for there is nothing for miles to make any sort of buzzing sound, other than rattlesnakes. Cousin Randy and I have sat up in those rocks for hours before, in July, with sweat just pouring off of us, even when we were motionless—especially when we were motionless—losing so much water that it was startlingly similar to thinking we had sprung a leak somewhere (Could this be fatal, we wondered? Yes!), and we have tried for hours at a time—one, two, three—to try to decipher the buzz, because it is trying to tell us something, the deer pasture is. There's no way you can hear the buzz and think anything else. It's a cryptic message. It tastes of wagon wheels and arrowheads and pioneer days. Hearing it, you cannot help but wonder.

We asked Howard about it once.

"What buzz?" he asked. But of course. He's never lived anywhere else. How can we expect him to compare it to anything else? The silence of Boston or the non-buzz of Houston—these things would toy with his old mind. He'd go racing back to Gillespie County immediately. I know he would.

"Nothing," we said. "It must have been a rattler."

So anyway, there we were, two dumb college kids, shirtless, moving up and down the pipeline, straining, rolling boulders the size of black Labs up and down the hill.

Howard wanted his house on the top of the hill. Where he could look down and see everything.

There's Rick, flipping over a rock and getting stung by a scorpion. There's Cousin Randy, smashing his finger between two big squares of the cabin. There's Howard, coming up the hill to see how they are doing. No, he didn't bring any lemonade, didn't bring any ice water, no beer, even. He says he forgot. Cousin Randy asks him how much water he has in his radiator.

See the cedar chips fly; see the cement harden. See the first row of stones rise, and then the second, and then the third. See Rick and Cousin Randy celebrate when they reach window level. See Rick and Cousin Randy go run down the mountain and dive into the waterfall pool below

Camp Creek. See them come bursting back up from the bottom of their dives, and shake the water from their hair, and feel the hot sun, and look up into the hot dizzying blue Texas Hill Country air, and see the cactus, and the mountains, and the cedars, and the granite boulders, and the swimming hole they are splashing around in. See them think: This is absolutely Heaven.

See the hawk spinning lazily high above them on a hot, dry plume of Hill Country updraft, thinking red-tailed hawk thoughts.

Nothing was out of synchrony. It was a perfect Hill Country afternoon. Everything was as it should be.

You get these feelings a lot at the deer pasture. In fact, you can get them just any old time you want to; all you have to do is stop and look around, and notice things, and you will realize that everything is just scheming right along. It is a closed system, still operating—oblivious to blunder, immune to disharmony.

You could no more tell the deer pasture that there are crimes going on in Houston than you could an astronaut that Apollo Eight didn't really land on the moon, that it was done in a Hollywood studio.

You'd be laughed off the premises.

Perhaps that is what the buzz is: laughter. Not sage wisdom, but mere, happy laughter. Child's laughter at the goodness of everything working together, like clockwork— a thousand miracles, all simultaneous: dragonflies flitting, bullfrogs snapping, rain falling, wind blowing, deer browsing. . . .

This is not to say that Cousin Randy and I, or any of us, can not learn from the coded child-laughter, if that is what it is. Rather, perhaps this means we can learn more than we had ever dared hope for. Perhaps this is one of the greatest lessons of all to be learned on the deer pasture.

It would be nice to catch the buzz-laughter in a bottle, take it back to the cities, sprinkle it from door to door, neighborhood to neighborhood, and be given ticker-tape parades, have Nobel Peace prizes awarded in our honor for our magic of goodness. . . .

It took us six weeks to finish the cabin. The roof was hard, but it was the chimney that held us up the most. Howard wanted it in the center of the cabin.

We had to be finished by mid-August; we had been planning for months to go rafting on the Colorado the third week of August. We started working by the light of the moon during the fourth week when it became apparent we were behind schedule. It was a full moon, that fourth week; it was like daylight, but even more; it was like that super-illuminated moment you see when a burst of lightning lights up the darkness. Only there was no flickering; it was that continuous kind of glow. We grinned at each other a lot. We could look at our watches and tell what time it was without shading our hands over the crystal. Nine o'clock, midnight, two, four-thirty. We grinned a lot. It was like being in a museum after hours; we felt like curators. We went down to the old rock house when the sun came up and had Howard scramble us up a dozen eggs and a skillet of sausage and potatoes. It was a beautiful morning. We slept on his porch, in the shade, on the plank flooring, until eleven-thirty. By noon we were hoisting rocks again.

The neat thing about Howard is this: he doesn't caution you to slow down. He just started cooking us breakfast every morning. And he started bringing us beer. Cold canned beer from town, not his nasty, wicked, homemade stuff.

He is a man of many talents. The country demands it.

Another thing about Howard: he never sweated. He'd sit there on his heels, hunkered down like a baseball catcher, and watch us, sometimes for hours, not saying a lot, just watching.

There wasn't a whole lot else to do in July.

I believe it was the highlight of his year.

And the rock house grew.

By the fifth week the chimney was finished. Cousin Randy and I were used to the buzz in the afternoons, and the moon went black, and at night the stars were like flecks of bright gold, and we worked by lantern-light. It was like being in a different country. Some nights there was heat lightning to the south, and night thunder. Once, we smelled rain, but never got any; the wind just blew a lot.

It was such a good smell. It was balmy; we had to wear jackets. We heard a bobcat, saw the skunk family out in the meadow on top of the Burned-Off Hill, and jumped a covey of quail coming down the hill back to Howard's house right before daylight, right at that darkest part of the night. The quail scared the tar out of us.

Quail roost on the ground, in what is called a roseate formation, in a circle, each one facing out, like a wagon train under Indian attack, and when they flush, it is like the petals of a blossom unfolding. Unfolding very rapidly, and with much noise.

Cousin Randy was in front; he screamed. He stepped right in their midst and woke them up. I laughed, until I jumped another covey myself about a hundred yards down the hill, in a lower meadow.

Our hearts were still tripping when we lay down for a nap on the back porch that morning, just as the sky began

to glow in that magic spot to the east. For breakfast, when we got up, we had ham and biscuits and grits and red-eye gravy and real eggs. I saw the eggshells in the garbage, and they were brown.

We hauled rocks, slapped chat, planed, hewed, mortared, cracked chinks, smoothed, hauled timber. There were never enough rocks. Gloves became a part of us.

If you think it feels good to slip your hunting boots off after a long day, you haven't lived 'til you've you've slipped a pair of sweaty old gloves off after wearing them all day.

The skylight was Cousin Randy's idea.

"To let the moon in, of course," he said.

It was still a new moon, and we couldn't test its position very well, but we remembered from other nights where it hung at nine o'clock, so in Howard's bedroom we put the skylight in the roof so he could see the moon while he was lying in bed, and then, because you couldn't see it from the kitchen, we put one there too.

It was pleasing, to think of him seated at the old wooden chopping-block-that-was-his-breakfast-table that sat in the middle of his kitchen and on which he cut up deer and turkey steaks as well as rolled biscuit dough and cleaned fish from the creek. Sitting there at three in the morning, unable to sleep, looking up through the skylight. Just an old man and the moon.

It took a little extra effort, but when we were through, as is always the case, we were glad we had done it.

We took our sleeping bags up there and tested it out.

At seven-thirty the moon was flat on the horizon, level with the top of the hill, spinning in through his curtains. It rose fast: at eight-thirty, sure enough, you could see it framed in the bedroom ceiling, like a picture. Then, like a ghost passing over, it moved on, across the cedar-slatted roof—quietly, quickly—before appearing, almost with an air of grinning, childish flamboyance, in the kitchen shortly before three.

We spent the whole night there that night, the night we finished. We were exhausted, dead asleep by ten, but even with a quarter moon and our fatigue, the change from darkness to light when the beams began to come spilling into the kitchen was so severe that it woke us anyway.

The next day, we put shutters on the skylight and rigged up a long pole that you could draw and open them with. We began moving Howard's stuff up the hill in the jeep: pot-bellied stove, glass collection, iron bed, dresser, everything.

You learn a lot about a person when you move him.

We learned that Howard was lonely. He had kept the mail addressed to Occupant. Some of it was quite old, for

products we'd never heard of, things so off-the-market and out-of-date that it made us dizzy just to hold the envelopes.

We found out that he was sentimental. There were bullet casings from lucky shots, turkey feathers he'd found while walking down in the creek bottom, and arrowhead chips and pieces, with a few whole ones—things he didn't really need, could get along without, but would enjoy having. Things that made his life a little fuller. Things like sky-lights in his cabin, in Gillespie County, to let the hunter's moon in, even in the summertime.

So now Howard lives up on the hill—not a Hudson Mountain of a hill, but still higher up than he was when he started, eighty-three years ago. He says when he was a kid, he lived down in the creek bottom. Then he moved to Camp Creek, where he stayed for sixty-nine years.

Now he is atop the Burned-Off Hill.

Gets a little closer to the moon with each move, he does.

It is an excellent strategy.

4
The Day Before

GRANDMOTHER Robson makes the best fried chicken in the world.

This is the excuse I use to pass through her town on the way to Gillespie County in the fall, the second week before Thanksgiving. It is not too terribly out of the way.

The thing you see right before you get to her house (if you are coming out of the north, as I do from Mississippi) is the mercury-vapor lamp. And if you have left the office at straight-up five o'clock on a Friday, it will be two A.M. the next morning when you see this light. It always casts the same goldish green glow over the railroad tracks and over the gravel road and over the fields beyond that.

Grandma Robson lives by herself out in the country; you have to cross the tracks to get there. At that time of night, there are never any trains out. They come at midnight and at dawn, but in all the seasons that I have been detouring through La Grange on my way to Gillespie County on the night before the opening day of white-tail season, I have never heard or seen even a trace of a train. It has gotten to where I do not even look anymore; I crest a hill, the mercury light comes in view, the tracks clump-ca-latter under my car, and I am there.

Grandma Robson has a screen porch with a screen door; that is another thing I remember, the sound the screen door makes. It is a sound everyone remembers, from different places. Sometimes I will hear a screen door slam in Jackson and it will actually confuse me to look

around and not see her or her fried chicken or her famous
Dr. Pepper bread, which I may have failed to mention but
is even better than her fried chicken. The screen door is
also a part of each year's hunt.

These are some of the other parts:

The sound the echo in the stairwell makes as I dash
out of my office at five and hurry down to the parking
garage, in far too much of a hurry to wait on the elevator.

The Tensas River. I always pass it right at dusk. Unless
it is raining, or real cold, there are always fireflies. Sometimes there are bats flying low across the river, but I never
slow down to watch.

Zwolle, Louisiana. I sometimes get a warning ticket in
Zwolle, but it is always just a warning ticket, because I am
never driving all that fast, just a little fast, and also because
the sheriff of Zwolle used to go deer hunting opening day in
the Texas Hill Country himself, in Gillespie County if you
can believe my luck; he understands. That is another thing
I remember—what it is he tells me each time he stops me.
He tells me to go a little more careful and to shoot a big one
for him.

I always go more careful.

The Coke machine in Shiro, Texas. Shiro is one hundred and twenty-one miles from La Grange; Shiro is getting close. Shiro is straight-up midnight; Shiro is where I
always start to nod and see things in the road when they
aren't really there.

Shiro has a population of two hundred and one; the
Coke machine in Shiro is outside a little country store
(closed down for the night many, many hours ago, of course)
and glows a cheerful red and white in the black East Texas
woods. I remember, too, the clunk! sound the bottle makes
as it slides down the chute, and the renewed, drugged-up
giddy feeling I get that carries me through for the rest of
the trip. La Grange is about two hours from Shiro; I slide

through the night on into Round Top, where I stop and dial her phone number from a pay phone.

It's a dirty trick, I suppose, but I'm a poor boy and can't afford a real call. I let the phone ring once, hang up, get in the car, and drive on. In La Grange, Grandma Robson hears the phone ring and gets up and starts fixing breakfast. Dr. Pepper bread, too. I wish I could give you the recipe, but as is the case with all worthwhile things, there isn't one.

She looks out the window as she waits, to see if the moon is bright. Full moons in Texas, she knows, are bad for deer hunters; the deer gorge on the Hill Country acorns all night and then sleep all day. They hole up in cedar brakes on the sides of mountains. They become invisible. Sometimes, if you are lucky, you will hear one kick a rock as he slinks away from your presence, your scent (if you are ambitious enough to enter the thickness of the cedars), but this is rare. Usually they just sort of disappear. The best thing to do if there is a full moon the night before is to use a two-man drive that next day.

One man on top of the mountain, having come up the north side—the side the deer aren't on in November—should very quietly walk along the top of the mountain, while the other man sits up in some rocks along the creek at the bottom of the mountain. The driver should not clack rocks or shake trees. He should stalk the mountaintop as quietly as possible. The deer will hear him.

Gillespie County white-tails are bad that way. They'll smell him or they'll sense his body heat, or they'll hear his heart pounding, or whatever it is they do that makes them so wary—that's what they'll do. They'll rise silently and slowly, without looking back, and begin to move down the mountain. If you're in the right place, with binoculars of course, you might see a glimpse of a shadow moving through the dark cedars. That has happened to me only once in four years of hunting. Usually they just seem to vaporize.

They stop when they reach the creek; they'll parallel it, still walking slowly, looking almost nonchalant.

Research biologists have discovered that after two or three minutes a white-tail will have forgotten what it is that spooked him; that except for his still-pounding heart and heightened senses of alarm, he will have forgotten what it was.

Their studies, of course, were not conducted in Gillespie County. I am firmly convinced that Gillespie County white-tails do not ever forget.

Breakfast is ready just as I drive up. There's not really time, but I always make time. Grits, biscuits, sausage, fried eggs, milk and orange juice. She fresh-squeezes the orange juice. It's always in that short little frosted glass with the chip in the lip. I don't know what I'd do if one year it was in a paper cup.

On an opening-day Gillespie County white-tail hunt, tradition is as important as anything, perhaps even more important than the deer. She tells me what the acorn crop is like as I eat. She runs out and checks the oil, thumps my tires; it's like a pit stop. She puts the fried chicken in a huge Tupperware bowl, a barrel really, and an extra loaf of Dr. Pepper bread in the front seat. She tells me she wishes she could go. She wishes me luck.

I suppose, after I leave, she goes back to bed.

I bet a lot of us hunters forget this sometimes, forget about the pit crew. I think every hunter has at least a small one; I'm a rogue renegade bachelor with no family in Mississippi, with as small a pit crew as anyone, yet I do have one. Grandma Robson's the head of it, of course, but there are other, less-publicized supporting members: my boss, who puts up with occasional yawns and minor tardiness during the hunting season; various hunting partners, who,

though they'd never tell me if they saw a big buck, do go out of their way to let me know when they hear of good sales on shotgun shells, camouflage clothing, etc. Everybody, I am convinced, has at least a partial pit crew. I feel fortunate that my own small one is one of the best.

On hunts like a Gillespie County white-tail season opener, tradition, as I have mentioned, is paramount. It's an important factor that cannot be over-rated, one which most sportsmen are aware of. This is not necessarily a true statistic, it's something I just made up, but if I was in a deep and heated argument I bet I could say this and no one would bat an eye: "National studies show that fully seventy-nine percent of the hunters polled have spent opening day of deer season in the same place for the last five years."

They find a good place, and they stick with it. Some years they may not have a good year, others, superb, but the more they return to such a place, the more good things they remember, and the more they stay. They may, and likely do, range, over the length of a season, but for opening day it's our affinity for traditions that makes that seventy-nine percent of us pick a favorite spot.

This may be blasphemous; you might say, "He's not a real deer hunter, not with an attitude like that; he's just an old butterfly collector," but I firmly believe my crowd—and they are a bunch of deer hunting sons-of-guns—would hold opening day deer camp in the J. C. Penney's parking lot if that's what it took to get us all together.

Day Two would be a different story, of course—there's nothing as sad and desolate as an empty freezer in camp that first night as the creek begins to freeze and grey dusk falls—but to our gang, I really believe the tradition is as important as the venison.

All paths converge in Gillespie County. While I am senselessly wandering downtown Jackson on my lunch break, like a rabid hound looking for a place to hide, just roaming up and down the sidewalks in the bright November Mississippi sun, trying to bleed off some of the energy, the others are calmer, closer. Their pre-hunt traditions are not nearly as frantic. By the time I am racing through the East Texas gloom, racing down lonely black-topped two-lane back roads that track in straight lines like funnels through the heavy pine forests, driving with the brights on to keep on the lookout for deer crossing the road, the rest of the Bass gang is already in camp.

I envy them; they've told me about their own pre-hunt traditions, or rather, I've interrogated them, and they seem much more relaxing than my mad-dog ditherings. I suspect they take their traditions for granted, but I also know that this does not diminish their enjoyment of them.

Grandaddy Bass shuts the gas station down at noon and drives back to the house to pack the truck. There's a gravel road that winds up through the hills out into the

country before crossing a river and turning downhill into
Fort Worth; it's a country gas station, and I know he takes
that gravel road every day. He hasn't told me this, but I
suspect that the way the rocks chink! chink! up against the
undercarriage is a part of his tradition on that special day
before.

He's got an icebox in his store, one of the old kind that
says "Coca-Cola" on the side of it. He keeps soft drinks in it
for customers. I happen to know for a fact that the last thing
he does before locking up on that day before is reach in that
icebox and get a strawberry soda pop and take it with him,
whether the weather is hot or cold, and he drinks it as he
drives. I know this because it's what he's always done; I re-

member seeing him do it even when I lived back in Texas, when I was too little to go on the hunt.

I know he thinks ahead to seeing us all there together, all his sons and grandsons—I know this because he's told me. I know he looks forward to beating us all badly in dominoes in the evenings when the cabin windows are shut and the glass panes rattle while the wind blows and the rain falls.

We stay there a week; there's always an ice storm at least one night.

Of course, he beats us when it's not storming and screaming-wind-and-black-inky-darkness outside, too; he beats us when the night sky is spring soft and it's warm and clear out, the kind of night when Cousin Randy and I often quit early and go up on the Big Granite Mountain to look at the stars. He beats us year in and year out. Tradition.

On those warm and clear springlike nights, those shirt-sleeve nights, the Big Granite Mountain—a bare dome, void of vegetation, nothing but beautiful pink gran-

ite polished by time—shines like a capitol dome under the
light of the stars and moon and looks pale and silver con-
trasted to the rest of the darker surrounding country. On
those nights we can always hear the sound of the Pedernales River. Somehow it always sounds the same, dry years
and wet, and from the little yellow squares of light in the
cabin below we can hear, if the night calm is still enough,
the sharp staccato clap-clap-clap sound of dominoes being
played against the linoleum table. We can hear the shouts,
the hoots, the happy laughter of the Bass men. The sounds
of tradition.

Dad and Uncle Jimmy and Cousin Randy come up
from Houston, or sometimes, if Randy's off somewhere—
Montana, Florida, Baja California—Dad and Uncle Jimmy
just come up by themselves. Brothers. They drive Uncle
Jimmy's car, and pull the jeep on the towbar behind them,
loaded to the gills with empty ice chests, hunting equipment, lanterns, and groceries. Dad and Uncle Jimmy
always buy the groceries. Boy, do they always buy the
groceries.

Weight is gained, on these Gillespie County deer
hunts. Oh yes.

They've made forty such hunts together. Not always
leaving from Houston like they do now, but always arriving
at the same place. Once Uncle Jimmy left a company golf
tournament in Tokyo a day early, flew all night, made some
horrible connections in Atlanta, and got in right at dawn,
but he made it.

Cousin Randy's the freest of the free spirits. It should
be said to his credit, however—if being a free spirit is a dis-
credit—that he always makes it. I am not sure what his tradition is; it may be the look on his boss's face when he tells
yet another one that he is quitting that day so he can go
deer hunting in Texas with the boys, or it may be the

simple way the rusted old key lock clicks in the darkness when he drives in on the ranch road a few hours ahead of me. I don't know. There's no idea what Cousin Randy's idea of tradition is, but whatever it is, I'll bet it's neat. Cousin Randy is all right.

They're all all right—the whole pit crew.

They're part of the tradition.

5
Cousin Randy

THEY are the field goal kickers of the outdoor world, the left-handed painters in a world of right-handed computer programmers. Edsels in a world of Fords and Chevrolets, every one of them. They are eccentric. They stand out above the blandness of the rest of society like a beacon, like a monument to all that is odd and bizarre and unorthodox and different. For entertainment, instead of playing video games or sleeping, they hunt ducks. They stalk deer, they fish through the ice, they shoot bows and arrows. Grown men and women, it is true, but I have caught dozens of them doing these very things.

I do not need to catch them at it, however; I have seen the symptoms so often, learned even the slightest facial tics and mannerisms so well, that I can upon meeting one identify a person immediately (without a single spoken word passing between us) as an Outdoorsman or an Other. It is that simple, that clear cut. There are no mixtures. Either they are or they aren't.

There are clever little tricks I have picked up on over the years to help me. I can, for instance, tell just by looking at a scar on a man's hand whether it was put there by an angry bird dog or an irascible typewriter. You would be amazed at the ease with which I can discern L-shaped barbed-wire rends in clothing and O-shaped fishhook rips from similarly shaped patches received in far less adventuresome pursuits such as cutting the grass and falling out of hammocks. A mere glance is all I need to confirm a sour

smile as being sour because the Big One got away or because the frowner ran over a nail on the way to work. At
fifty paces I can tell what kind of a campfire the Outdoorsman built the night before and how long he stood
by it. I have learned these things through experience; I
can tell.

And once he opens his mouth, there is no doubting.
The conversation of an Outdoorsman is as different from
that of Others as a solunar table is from a breakfast table.
When in tall, crowded buildings, parking garages, shopping
centers, and dark restaurants, Outdoorsmen look dazed and
confused, even vacant, and fidget before speaking of such
esoteric and erstwhile matters as the great ice storm of
ought-eight and the true function of the posteriorly posi-
tioned dorsiventral fins on spawning cutthroats. The conversation of an Other is far less entertaining, far less amus-
ing; he can usually be heard discussing such drivel as the
energy shortage, inflation, and other simplistic and irrelevant insignificances. He is at home in tall crowded buildings and parking garages; he likes shopping centers and
dark restaurants.

The dress of Outdoorsmen often differs slightly from
that of Others, but I will not delve into that here. It is safe
to say that an Outdoorsman would never dream of embarrassing a host or hostess by overdressing; Outdoorsmen are
very considerate in this regard.

They are all different; they are all the same. They love
the outdoors as they love themselves. They are into clear
mountain streams, snowshoeing, aspen leaves in the fall
and birchbark canoes. They are not into crime, vandalism,
drugs, and strip mines. They would rather see the great
white glaciered teeth of the Tetons sawing up through the
clouds on a wintry Wyoming morning than the vast and impressive planar spread of a downtown parking lot; they
would rather see the vast and impressive planar sprawl of a

southern Utah desert in purple twilight than a tall and ma-
jestic skyscraper sawing up through the fog of a downtown
Manhattan on a blustery February evening.

Sometimes they are tall, sometimes they are short,
but in the sense that Henry David Thoreau used the word,
to connote that which is associated with wilderness, they
are all one thing: wild. I'm sure you all know one, at least,
and maybe have had the good fortune to hunt with one. It
seems as if they were made for that kind of life—hunting.
It makes you feel good about yourself, just seeing them enjoy that kind of life so much. Cousin Randy is my brush
with this kind of wildness.

Randy had a girl friend once, up in Utah, where I believe he went to undergraduate school (Cousin Randy's past
is not always clear in spots, but rather is punctuated by
vague and fuzzy gaps and patches about which he himself is
not really certain sometimes; Cousin Randy doesn't sweat
the little things). Her name was Sue Spurr, and she wore
sagebrush perfume and chamois shirts and hiking boots to
class and had rich brown hair that I know for a fact was the
color of dark honey in the sunlight, for I saw a picture of
her, and Cousin Randy fell in love with her instantly. She
was in his 8:30 economics class his freshman year and was
majoring in wildlife management.

This is the kind of man I go hunting with; this is how
my Cousin Randy is. For his first date with this Sue girl
they went duck hunting out in the marsh. She shot three
and he shot two. He tells me that he knew then he had
found someone special.

Besides being pretty, maybe even beautiful, Sue was
tough. In the winters, she ran cross-country for the girl's
track team, and in the summers she worked up in Wyoming on the Marlboro Man's ranch, digging postholes and
branding cattle and fishing in the stock tanks. For fun she
would walk through the sage and jump up jack rabbits and

chase them down and cuff their ears on a dead run. She'd have been hell, Randy said, on the armadillo population. Back in Utah, during school, she lived off campus by herself with a cat named Greenpeace.

Sue liked to do other things besides chase rabbits and hunt ducks, but not as much. The marsh they hunted in was a ten-minute drive from campus, down off the bench-like shelf of the Wasatch Mountains and out into the historic Cache Valley. If it was windy and snowing hard, it sometimes took them fifteen or twenty minutes extra. They took my cousin's motorcycle. This was before the advent of the great, red, thunderous, go-everywhere all-terrain three-wheelers that hunters are so fond of these days, but in many respects it resembled one: it had a sidecar.

Sue would sit down in the sidecar, all bundled up with goggles and heavy muffler and long hair flying, with the waders and ammo and all their decoys stowed down by her feet, holding the guns in her mittened hands, and Cousin Randy, also wearing a muffler and goggles, would straddle the old sand-blasted-grey horse of iron, feeling very suave, very dashing, very cold, and then off they would roar into the howling, frigid blackness of the Utah dawn. There was not room for them to wad both their waders down into the sidecar; Cousin Randy rode with his on.

She was easily the most beautiful girl in a school of fair-muscled but hard-wintered farming women, and Cousin Randy was the luckiest guy. Sometimes if it was not snowing they would take their mittens off and hold hands as they drove, but never for very long, and not very often. The cold blasts of the predawn winds washing over them made their hands lock, made their little fingers freeze into icy crooked J-shapes that refused to straighten out when the rest of their fingers did, which made it hard to blow a duck call or handle a shotgun. They were very dedicated, Randy told me; they saved most of their hand-holding for trout season. And kissing in the duck blinds was definitely out; one could never tell when a brief spell of ardor could be broken by the high, fast, wind-cutting whistle of incoming teal. They played it safe and saved the kissing for trout season, too.

First light generally came around 6 or 6:15. Monday through Friday they were able to hunt for a good two hours before gathering up their ducks and dashing back to class. They had no dog; there would not have been room for him in the motorcycle sidecar anyway. Those ducks that they could not wade out to, Sue would retrieve with expert casts of the fly rod they kept stashed away in the blind for that purpose. By charging down the highway, up the hill to campus, short-cutting through the cemetery, and overlanding across the great grassy snow-covered-during-duck-season quadrangle outside Old Main, scattering students walking to class to either side of the motorcar's mad rush, they were able to reach the economics building by 8:30.

They would drive right up to the front door, dismount on the run, kick the snow and slush from their boots, and rush inside, shotguns tucked under one arm and economics books under the other, still wearing their hunting clothes, duck decoys and calls draped around their necks, game bags warm and full, brimming with bright tufts of feathers that peeked out for the rest of the class to see (it was a big class; it was held in the auditorium), and with flushed cheeks and tingling noses they would clump down to the front seats, where they sat down just as the 8:30 bell was beginning to clatter.

Their professor never mentioned it to them once, never even suggested that they leave the dead ducks outside before coming to lecture. He, too, was a duck hunter; he understood.

It was not until Cousin Randy's junior year that she broke his heart by marrying an accounting student from

Appleton, Wisconsin. He was tall and thin and frail as a reed but owned two four-wheel-drive trucks and a black Lab named Jake and a hunting lodge up on the Minnesota-Canada border.

Cousin Randy told me that he kept the motorcycle, but, unable to stand the sight of it, separated the old sidecar from it and abandoned it out in a farmer's lonely wheat field a few miles south of town, on the main road leading out.

To this day yet, he tells me, he cannot hear the slow, pulsing idle of an old and poorly tuned motorcycle without feeling the hot tears of bittersweet nostalgia well up in his eyes. And trout season, I have noticed, makes him manic-depressive.

Sometimes Cousin Randy is not merely different; sometimes, he is also dangerous. It was Cousin Randy who came up with the novel approach to keeping our feet warm two hunts ago. After only the first day of the five-day hunt, our leather boots were soaking wet from hiking through two inches of snow all day long.

"I've an idea," said C. R. as we crawled into our down sleeping bags in the sleet-entombed cabin. "To keep our feet from being cold in the morning, let's leave our boots outside overnight." A light snow was beginning to fall.

For a moment my mind reeled. "Did you say, 'Leave our boots out overnight?'" I asked incredulously. It was mid-November. It was not supposed to get above freezing all week.

"The only reason our feet get cold is because they get wet. If we leave the boots outside, they'll freeze, and the water will be locked up in ice crystals; it won't be able to get us wet and therefore make us cold."

Right? Wrong. It didn't get us wet, but it very definitely made us cold. And that was one of his better ideas.

This is the same Cousin Randy who, after taking an

animal behavior class in college, suggested that I run through the cedars at the deer pasture waving a white handkerchief up and down, weaving a long and circuitous path about the premises before racing past his tree stand. According to theory, if I ran fast enough and stayed in heavy cover so that the deer couldn't get a good glimpse, they would see the white handkerchief flagging up and down and would all assume I was a startled deer. They would follow me, said Cousin Randy.

He is a persuasive speaker, and I am a poor listener; listening to him, and watching the impressively dramatic but totally irrelevant sweeping motions his arms and hands made, listening to the enthusiastic whoosh-crash! sounds he was making that were supposed to sound like an entire forest of panicked deer following my bobbing handkerchief, I was convinced.

This was before I got out of school and had to go to work for a living; I lived on some property my parents had down near Goliad. I trained for months. That is how I best remember Cousin Randy: sitting in a director's chair on a warm summer evening out in the country, dressed in sweats but completely at ease, a silver whistle on a cord draped around his neck, a notepad in his lap, the dusky grey mist of a summer fog down in the creek bottom a few miles from our farm. The evening's first few yellow blots of fireflies cruising far out over a meadow, and crickets. The evening's first hoot owl boom; the crunch of gravel under my feet as I ran and ran and ran and ran: uphill, downhill, backwards, and frontwards, with fifteen pounds of leg weights wrapped around my ankles. The total wetness of my sweat, even when it was not raining, and the blistered feet, the dust-seared lungs. I also remember the sadistic shrills of the whistle.

One shrill meant faster. Two shrills, further. Three shrills, faster and further. Most of the whistles came in threes. Cousin Randy never left the chair. He kept a pair of binoculars at his side, like a general, and would watch me through them whenever I got too far out of range to be seen with the unaided eye. Even when I was out of sight of the field glasses, off over a hill somewhere, collapsed in a cool, green, grassy meadow, gasping for breath, even then I could hear the whistle, blowing in grim bursts of threes. He was highly dedicated.

Opening day found me crouched beneath his blind— we had told no one about the plan—lacing up my tennis shoes while he checked the safety on his rifle. I wore gym shorts and gloves and a long-sleeved grey flannel sweatshirt; a light snow was falling—it seemed that a light snow was always falling around Cousin Randy—sprinkling the woods with a silent white dusting that sparkled and looked almost magical. The air tasted cold and clean and frosty; I felt I could run forever.

"Try to run through the brush," Cousin Randy's hushed whisper drifted down. "Try to make a lot of noise. Yell 'Hullabaloo, Caneck, Caneck' from time to time," he advised. Each time he spoke, puffy clouds of water vapor the color of milk leapt from his mouth. His hands were mittened; his neck was scarved. He was wearing long underwear. I nodded, hitched up my shorts, and was off.

The snow sprayed up around my ankles and got in my socks as I ran, but I didn't mind; I was in shape. I could go all day. I flashed the handkerchief in the air like it was on fire. "Hullabaloo, Caneck-Caneck!" I shouted, crashing through downed timber the way a panicked deer might. "Hullabaloo, Caneck-Caneck!" I shouted as loud as I could. I was vaguely aware of passing by Grandaddy's stand, but it was hard to tell; it was still early morning, and I was streaking through heavy cover with my head down and arms pumping. Once or twice I thought I heard shouts, but wasn't sure.

We read about ourselves in the newspaper the next day. The headlines, as they say, screamed. "Opening Day Local Deer Harvest Down; Some Blame Mysterious Wild Boy."

They had all of our gang's eyewitness accounts in there. Uncle Jimmy said it was a naked wolf-boy, running with a pack, and Dad said it was a tall fat man, as big as a football player in pads. Howard said it was a midget on horseback. Grandaddy said there was a whole gang of them, that there had to be, because he had looked out one window of his blind and had seen a strange hairless apelike creature running through the trees; when he looked out the other window, there was another one on the other side.

"They were everywhere," he was quoted as saying. He

swore that he personally had counted as many as twenty-three at one time. As I said, I was in very, very good shape. There was brief mention of the hullabaloo-caneck-canecking which most of our crowd had interpreted as some sort of wounded death cry; Uncle Jimmy had become frightened and had had to climb down from his blind and hurry back to

the cabin—we felt bad about that. Dad said he suspected it was some sort of Missing Link. Grandaddy said he thought it was a haint. When they interviewed Cousin Randy and me, we told them we had seen nothing.

It was a long hunt; we shot not a single deer that season. On the last day, after it was over, and after the cold, grim realization of an empty freezer had sunk in, Cousin Randy tried to run away from me, but I was faster and could run further. I caught up with him and beat his little silver whistle with a stone until it was as flat as a dime. Then I hurled it into the woods like a man skipping a stone across a wide, flat lake. Cousin Randy stood there, wheezing slightly, looking off in the direction he had last seen his whistle headed.

"Well, look at it this way," he said, eyeing nervously the stone I had crushed his whistle with and was still gripping. "At least we're in shape."

That is the kind of cousin I have. That is the kind of person I go hunting with on my Gillespie County deer hunts each fall.

6

More About Cousin Randy

EVER brush your teeth with Ben-Gay? Wake up with a ter-rified armadillo in your sleeping bag? No? You've obviously never been deer hunting with Cousin Randy.

Sometimes he does this: he peels the labels off all our canned foods so that each meal has an aura of mystery about it. Beans for breakfast, tomato sauce for supper. He laughs.

Whenever anyone in camp gets sprayed by a skunk, it's always Cousin Randy.

Grandaddy's been to camp forty-nine years. He's never been sprayed by a skunk. Uncle Jimmy's been forty-six times. No skunk sprays for him. Dad, forty-four hunts. No skunks. Even I am ahead: Rick, four; skunks, zero.

Cousin Randy has been to camp for four years now. He's been sprayed thirteen times. Actually, that's mis-leading—he's really only been sprayed on eight different occasions, but on the last time, he got sprayed by six skunks at once: a mother and five babies.

This year Randy's on probation. We warn him, but he just laughs. He does enjoy the deer pasture.

Grandaddy thinks he does it on purpose, to make him angry. And it's true, he's a little bad to Grandaddy sometimes.

Grandaddy's eyes aren't as good as they once were. This happens, I am told. Grandaddy shows up each year with a little stronger pair of glasses than before. Each year he shoots a little bigger deer than before; how, I have no

idea, but he does. Even when there are no big deer on the pasture that year, he'll find one.

There's something you need to know about dawn in the Hill Country, if you don't already.

A lot of times it's really foggy. I mean, socked in. The fog is thickest down in the creek bottoms, packed thick, a soft, smoky, inpenetrable grey, but even to the person moving up the slopes, through the cedars, it is like being inside a cloud, sort of dreamy, and up top, on the mesas, even as the sun is coming up and spinning the meadow fog off—lighting it up in a gold glow and sending it scurrying

for the creek bottoms—the mountains and hills and high places take on a watery sort of pastel look, bathed in fuzzy clean new color. There is a sort of quiet, happy feeling, a celebration, sort of, every time the sun comes up on a foggy morning and does that. It's like a welcome back.

The deer like those foggy mornings, because it extends their feeding period a little further past dawn. They feel a little safer, a little more invisible, and in November, with their winter coats tan grey and their antlers polished bone, they are. They move a little further out into the meadows and cut up a little more. They dance, rear up on their hind legs, and paw the air, boxing at each other, kangaroo-style. Spikes lower their heads, shake their little horns, and mock-charge each other. Grandaddy sits up in his blind, on the East Side, and watches this. He has, by seniority, the meadow. This is not the wildest spot on the deer pasture—he can't get to the wildest spots anymore—but it's the place where you're likely to see the most deer. There's a little creek that goes through the meadow, and a big bluff up on the north side that looks down over the meadow. The meadow's flanked on the south side by little granite hills and oak thickets. Grandaddy's blind is up in those oaks; looking out from inside it, you can see the creek flowing through the meadow from left to right, west to east, downhill. The deer usually file slowly down a series of switchbacks on the bluff, in the northwest corner of the meadow. You can see them down there sometimes, see their legs moving below the browse line, see their shapes and shadows. Sometimes an antler will glint in the morning sun.

Cousin Randy cut, out of plywood, with a saber saw, a trophy deer to end all trophies. A big one. The size of a small bull. He painted it grey, old grizzled grey, put white spots around the eyes and the nose, painted a white patch on the throat, and wired antlers to the head. A bunch of

antlers. About thirty-two points' worth of them. The thing looked like a moose. Grandaddy got very excited when the fog lifted and he saw it standing there on the other side of the meadow. He adjusted his glasses, eased up in his blind, and fired twenty-four times.

You could hear the gunshots all over the deer pasture, but also you could hear Cousin Randy's hoots of laughter, a good half-mile away, all the way over on the back side of Buck Hill.

He is so bad.

7
Uncle Jimmy

ONE year, when Charlie, my father, was at the getting-wide-in-the-shoulders age—fifteen, sixteen, could have been seventeen, even—he climbed up in Howard's old hay barn, up in the loft, and roped a deer. Pure and simple. There was a little buck that came and raided Howard's garden every morning: nibbled corn, grazed on radishes, browsed the grapes. Very insolent. So Charlie got a little bucket of corn nubbins and sprinkled them, as if in a fairy tale, in a trail leading from the garden to a point in the barn directly beneath the hayloft, where he spent the night.

He said he could see the lights of the cabin, down on the creek, and could hear occasional hoots and shouts drift up the canyon from the domino game. It must have been lonely. Only during the rubbing-one's-horns-on-the-trees stage of one's life would one do such a thing. The grey sky in the east woke him. From the hayloft he must have had quite a panoramic view. Sunrise in the Hill Country is silently spectacular. It can't be too far off from how the first sunrise ever looked.

Charlie sat up, wiped the sleep from his eyes, and mussed the hay from his hair. Yawned, but didn't wish for coffee. Young bucks in the tree-rubbing stage, in the Hill Country, don't need it. The deer was coming Charlie's way. Charlie could hear the square little teeth grinding on the corn nuggets. It sounded like a dog clacking on a bone. He got his rope ready, already coiled, and leaned out over the loft. The deer paused right under him. Charlie threw

the rope and lassoed it around the antlers. Pulled tight. The deer went berserk, pulled tighter. Almost pulled Charlie out of the hayloft. He had to very quickly tie one end of the rope off on an overhead beam. Then he climbed down and ran back down the hill to camp. He had breakfast, a big one; didn't tell anyone what he'd done. Had seconds on the biscuits.

Up on the hill, Howard came out and saw the deer thrashing around in his front yard.

"Charlie," he said, just the one word, the way he might look up in the sky and say "rain" or "snow." He shook his head. He cut the deer loose; the deer ran off. Never came back to the garden again.

Grandaddy's only told that story once.

Here's a story of my own. This is for true a real one; I saw it happen. I didn't believe it at first, but it did happen. Uncle Jimmy was mighty embarrassed that I saw it. The whole thing, from start to finish.

I was walking across the middle of the Burned-Off Hill

when it happened. Now I know you're not supposed to
walk across the middle of any opening down on the deer
pasture, regardless of time of day or direction of wind, or
anything. If you do, everything can see you, and you can
see nothing.

So I was walking across the middle of the field. Daydreaming. I like walking through fields, see. I was just hop-
ing no one would see me. It would have been embarrassing
to try to explain that at that particular moment the one
thing in the world I felt like doing more than anything else,
more than shooting a deer even, was walking through that
field. Cousin Randy might have understood, but he'd have
been the only one. Thistles crunched and popped as I
walked. Grasshoppers sprang up in alarm and clacked away
in bright orange-and-black glides. My uncle leapt down out
of a tree at the other end of the pasture.

I stopped, blinked, gawked. He was shouting and
laughing and waving his arms. There were deer running
everywhere. One deer, an especially wild-eyed doe, nearly
ran me over.

If you think deer look fast running through the woods
at a distance, you should see them when they are really
close, say, ten, twenty yards away and moving out. It was
all blur and eyes; it was gone almost before I was through
seeing it.

Uncle Jimmy is fifty-eight years old. He wears a suit to
work. He has forty-one people, forty-two counting his
youngest son, Russell, working for him, and I can promise
you that not a one of them has ever seen him leap out of a
tree. Not even Russell. He, Uncle Jimmy, is just a little
overweight. I rather imagine that the tiny tree sagged as he
crouched up in it, waiting for those deer to come by. I forgot to mention this, but it was the only tree on top of the
whole Burned-Off Hill. Just a little runt of a scrub, really, a

stunted live oak. You've seen them. It probably wasn't any thicker around at the trunk than a big man's leg.

I walked over to where he was and confronted him.

"What are you doing?" I asked. He looked sheepish. It was very obvious that he had not thought anyone would see him. "Why did you jump out of that tree and scare all those deer?" I demanded. I was still incredulous; I could not believe I had seen it with my own eyes. Fifty-eight years old! An executive!

"I just felt like doing it," he said, defensively, but not at all weakly. Then he squared his chin a little more. "Yeah, that's it, I just felt like doing it."

Cousin Randy's father after all, for sure, beyond a shadow of a doubt.

But then again, maybe it's just the wind. At night it blows and comes in the cabin windows and washes down out of the rocks and tall places over on the East Side. Or it could be something in the water. Or the moon—that's it, it could be the moon. . . .

8
Why We Do It

BY now you may be beginning to suspect that we go to the deer pasture each November for reasons other than hunting deer, and it's true, but for a fact there is essentially one and only one thing that is thought about during the daylight hours, from first grey light to too-dark-to-see-through-the-scope dusk, or at least until we each have a deer in the freezer, and the thought is exactly that: getting one. Challenging. Winning. Making the kill, to put it bluntly. Harvesting, to put it to people who do not understand.

Please do not give credence to the people who tell you they hunt for the meat. It is true that everyone uses the deer they shoot; no one goes out and hunts deer just for the pleasure of killing them. It's too hard, for one thing; there are a lot easier things in the woods to hunt than white-tailed deer, if blood-lust death-killing-something is all that is desired. But to say that "I hunt for the meat" is misleading and defensive, and hunters have neither cause nor reason to be either of these. I doubt seriously that there is a hunter in the Texas Hill Country who has to kill a deer to survive. Who has to make the kill or die. Or who could not use the time spent deer hunting digging ditches instead, or working a garden, and buy with the wages earned or crops raised enough nondeer food to survive, or at least replace the deer he didn't hunt. People in the past have had to depend upon hunting deer to stay alive, and may yet in the future, but right now the year is 1985, and the state, Texas, and you can not tell me that this is not so and that anybody

who tells you otherwise is not just blowing smoke or flat-
out making up stories. Nobody hunts deer for the meat because they have to.

This does not mean that there are not people who use
the meat they kill; there are. Everyone does, and to a startling extent; there is no stockyard carcass cleaned as bare
and gleaned of meat as that of a white-tail hanging in deer
camp. One learns, senses immediately with the first shot,
the responsibility inherent in dispensing life and death—in
deciding to shoot or not to shoot—and after coming to such
a realization, the thought of waste as the result of such a
decision becomes anathema. It's not even just meat that's
used, but also antlers, hooves, bones, and hide. The hunting dogs get the rest. And most hunters—say, eighty to

ninety percent of them—like the taste of venison better than beef, it is true, and if they did not hunt deer they wouldn't be able to have it, so in a sense they do hunt for the meat, but not in the sense that bad things will happen if they don't get it. And some'll tell you that they do it to help keep the herd population in balance, and this is true, too. I know lots of hunters, ever increasing numbers of hunters, who do just that —shoot does instead of bucks, spikes too, trying to help balance the population of herds they are familiar with—and these are all good excuses, if excuses were needed, but they are not reasons. They are near-reasons, which can be confused with reasons.

But the way to strip away all of the near-reasons, and get to the reasons, is this: Would they still hunt deer in the Texas Hill Country if those near-reasons didn't exist? If the meat wasn't as good as or better than beef? If the population wasn't balanced? Would they still hunt deer? And the answer is, of course, yes, and the reason is the challenge. The full freezer is icing, an added bonus. The reaffirmation of survival skills, the confidence obtained by deciding to try to go out and do something and then actually doing it— discovering a deer that does not want to be discovered, doing better than he at his own game in his own environment on his own home ground—winning—there is appeal to some in doing this, and this is why they hunt. This is the last variable that must be stripped away to explain the reason a man or woman hunts.

It is evident in the hunters who stop hunting. There are lots of them; nearly everyone knows one: a hunter, usually a great one, who just sort of gets away from it, doesn't stop hunting so much as he or she just stops harvesting. Starts sitting and watching more, and shooting less. Sometimes takes up photography. Begins to shoot maybe only one deer every other year or so. Does a *lot* of watching. Comes into camp in the evenings with tales for the other

hunters of a really *big* deer over on the East Side, as big as
he's ever seen on the place. Or comes in with no tales at all,
just all unused bullets and a good appetite from hiking and
being outdoors all day, and a cheerful, non-tense, relaxed
attitude. The challenge has waned; after *x* amounts of both
victories and failures, some mediocre, some spectacular,
the hunter is no longer in search of his abilities. He knows
that there are deer out there smarter than he and deer out
there that are dumber—that he is somewhere in between
most of them—but that what matters is not knowing where
the skill level and ability of those deer lie, but rather, his
own: his boundaries and capabilities and limits and defini-
tions; what is inside him; what makes him, the hunter, go.
    That is what deer hunting is, what few hunters realize
consciously but what paradoxically gives hunting its appeal;
it is not a hunt for the deer, an outside factor, but rather a
hunt for the hunter inside—a tracking of his own self. The
deer at the end of the tracking is incidental; it is only
the beauty of the outside natural world and surroundings
that masks this fact. Some people hunt geodes in the desert,
others perform plays in the city, while others build bridges,
design buildings—and like the deer-hunters, they may
never realize that it is not the plays and the bridges they
are chasing, but rather that these are merely points that
they are looking to and traveling toward as they move
along, growing older. It is at this point of realization, usually, that they retire from the stage, stop building bridges,
and begin photographing deer or just watching them instead of shooting them all the time. It takes some hunters a
single hunt to realize this; others, twenty; others, forty.
Some never recognize it, of course, and the bridges keep
getting built and the plays keep getting acted. But the
meat and the population dynamics are at the end of the
path; they are the destination, but they are not the unroll-
ing of the path itself, which is the person inside, which is
the real reason.

But ask the question, and they will answer something else, because unless they are looking very closely, or traveling very slowly, stopping and observing, that is all they can see when you ask them: the end of the path, rather than the path. The buck in the middle of the path at the end of the trail, his antlers shining golden in the morning sun: that is the obvious sight, but not the answer.

As with everything, getting there is almost always more important than there itself.

For some of us, it is an irresistible path to follow. The trick is not to try to resist following it, but rather to look around and observe once you are on it. It is a path of self, and a terrible waste not to recognize it as such.

The hardest deer I ever hunted, I never got; he won, I lost. I can accept this; it bothers me not. I went into the broken rocks and cedars and mountains and canyons back on the East Side, into his country, and he beat me. I came back out, and he stayed. I didn't give him a name. I don't know why I didn't; most of the time, when a hunter becomes involved with a trophy buck like this one, he'll attach some name to the creature, something to add personality, something inevitably corny like Old Mossy Horns, or the Big Twelve Point, or even Old Grey-Deer. I didn't, though; this deer was too smart even to be named. Naming implies mortality. It is that marvelous streak of human nature that makes it seem as if once an object has been named and defined, it can be had, be it a mathematical equation, a strain of cancer, or whatever, and this was just not the case with this deer. He was unhaveable.

Also, I had never seen enough of him at one time to name. I saw his rubs on the cedar saplings, saw glimpses of him running back in the cedars, glints of horns, the deep prints he made in the sandbars down on the creek, his dew claws sinking in up to his hock—but I never saw him square on, not enough to define him. Naming also implies knowledge, and I just flat didn't know this deer. I suppose if I was to call him anything, it would have been "The Shadow," or something like that. Because even on my best days, when I got up my earliest and stalked my quietest and hid down in the rocks my stillest—even then, that was all I ever saw, really, the shadows of the places he had been, and then I would do something really stupid like blink or breathe or even make my heart start beating, and he would hear it or see it, and he wouldn't be there; the dark form I had almost seen through the cedars would suddenly no longer be there, and I'd know he was gone.

Sometimes, even in the middle of the brightest days, there are canyons and deep thick scrubs of cedar on the slopes of the near-vertical bluffs back on the East Side that are dark as twilight, spooky to be in by yourself. It's a long way from camp; it's the point furthest from the cabin. You run into our fence line but cross it, as we did pig hunting one night, and you get over onto Mr. Edgar Gold's old place, up the creek about two hundred yards, and suddenly you find yourself in the depths of a cataclysmic, exploded, twisted, contorted mass of boulders and tilted-vertical rock formations called Hell's Half-Acre. I think this is where that deer was living when I was hunting him, but he liked to cross the fence and nap in the shade of our cedars sometimes on the hottest days. I do not really think he was honestly one of our resident deer, which made him all the more coveted, all the more desirable.

I hunted him two seasons. The closest I ever got to him was on the third day of the first year, the day when, coming back down the hill, scuffling through the live oaks, feet crunching leaves, head down, daydreaming, thinking about lunch, just grinning, grinning like a teenager in love, just happy to be there, I discovered him. The wind was just right; it was lifting lightly up out of the creek bottom, far below, and he was on the mid-slope, napping.

He must have thought I was a whole herd of deer, I guess, moving slowly through the dead, dry oak leaves, or a cow, maybe, a big, slow, stupid, upwind and odorless cow. He knew I wasn't a hunter; hunters, he knew, tip-toed, or crept around semifurtively on the balls of their feet and clacked rocks and broke twigs every thirty steps or so, and then froze with fear after making such mistakes. Hunters, he knew, did not come sailing straight down the middle of the woods with not a thought in their heads.

As I have said, it was my first year to hunt the deer pasture.

I rather like to imagine the flat out-and-out alarm, consternation, and even rage, yes, rage—No fair! You're supposed to play by the rules! You're not supposed to make noise on purpose—that flared up in his eyes and in his mind when, with sickening stomach and lurching heart, he realized that I was neither herd of deer nor cow after all, but hunter, and that I was within rock-throwing distance of him before he discovered it.

I really was, I was almost upon him. I had left the oaks, gone across the meadow, and was down in the cedars, in his cedars, when I saw him.

I like to think it is the closest any human being has ever gotten to him.

I know it is the closest.

I could see the sleekness of his coat, and how golden butter tan it was, even in the shadows, where the few soft bars of sunlight that did shaft down through the overstory struck him, and I remember thinking, in a detached sort of way, how very odd it was that a deer that size should have such a light and golden coat; usually, in the Hill Country, the really big bucks have a darker coat, a light slaty color, even, sometimes. I remember thinking how oddly instinctive it was to be swinging my rifle up and putting the scope on him, smoothly, without thinking, as if there was a voice inside me going through all the steps involved, and that it was not me at all, but some deeper, ancestral urging, saying be calm, poise, raise, strike, harvest. I remember going through these motions calmly, confidently. I remember seeing the big deer crash straight through a row of wind-felled timber, branches popping and limbs snapping, giving it all or nothing, literally smashing his way through a wall of logs and dead cedar, and then for a long, long time I could continue to hear his mad escape, and I remember thinking, well, if he had stayed around another four or five seconds, I would have shot him and killed the biggest buck Grandaddy had ever seen, the biggest buck ever killed in Gillespie County. I remember not being disappointed until about fifteen minutes later, walking on back to camp again, when, after getting over the initial marvel of just seeing such a magnificent creature, I began to mourn the fact that I had not gotten lucky, as they say, and beaten him. Won. Returned to camp the victor. The provider. Cries of excitement and adulation from the tribesmen. Hoopla and kudos and meat for a month, for all of us.

I somehow conveniently overlooked the fact that I had been lucky as stink just to have seen the big deer in the first place.

That was really the last time I ever saw him at all, running or otherwise. I haunted those cedars, hid everywhere imaginable. I stayed up in my hammock, twelve feet high, one night, to see if he moved through there at night when the moon was big. Anything, to try to pin him down for even a little clue, a little information into his private life. But he was unhuntable; he refused to participate.

I wasted a lot of time over on that mountain in those cedars and learned a lot about white-tails. Saw a lot of other deer. It's an interesting concept, going into an area and then just living there, practically, and paying intense and minute attention to every detail, learning it like, as they say, the back of your hand, and essentially forsaking all other areas—the Water-Gap, the Old Moss Tree, Buck Hill, the Pipeline. . . . I don't do it anymore; I wander everywhere, sort of taking the whole pasture in smorgasbordlike, but those first two years, with the memory of that big monster still exciting me every time I thought of him, I camped. I stuck tight to the very place I'd seen him. I became a student of that spot.

The closest I ever got to him again was the first day of my second season. He had gone back to the cedars; I was sitting there when the sun came up that first morning, sitting on a rock with both arms wrapped around me, breathing out smokeclouds even through my nose, and wondering what I could do about it. There was no way to make them turn invisible; you could see them a mile off— puff, puff. . . puff, puff. . . . I felt as if I was doing as much good as if I had been jumping up and down and shouting

"Here I am! Here I am!"—when I saw that he was watching me. He was crouched down and motionless, like a wary thing, more like a feral dog or coyote than a deer. He was about thirty yards downslope, and he was behind some cedars along a little ridge of granite that ran at about a forty-five degree angle down the slope, through the cedars, and on across the creek and up another hill. He was watching me. I know now, I think anyway, that it was my imagination, but at the time, his eyes looked golden. Like a Weimaraner's, like a Labrador retriever's; they did not look like the eyes of a deer, and they did not blink. It was spooky. I think now it was just the morning sun coming up over my back. Back in the cedars, he was really just more of a silhouette than a form. You could see him frozen there, studying me, evaluating me; you could see him weighing his options.

I watched his shadow watch me; you could see it was against his character to go charging wildly off into the brush when frightened, as did most other white-tails. As he did the first time he saw me. You could tell it was against his character to be frightened, too. He was not a panicky deer.

What he did was this: he sank down to his belly, down to the ground, so that he was behind that ridge of rock that ran through the new growth of cedars. Was it a fault scarp? The remnants of an old stone fence from settler days, or older? An eroded, exposed volcanic intrusion? Whatever it was, it was between two and three feet high, and sinking down behind it was like hiding behind a rock wall. A rock wall that ran all the way down the slope, to safety. All he had to do was make it down to the creek, crawling, of course, like a commando on hands and knees; but surely he wouldn't do that. Deer don't have minds like that, capable of understanding such abstract concepts as strategy and planning and the like. That deer wasn't able to look at the rock wall and know that if he stayed behind it, and stayed

down, I couldn't see him. At best, he was probably sitting there, terrified, frozen, waiting for me to do something, something that would trigger his instinct and allow him to react. Deer, and other animals like them, are different from people; they merely react; they can't think, can't map out escape strategies. I knew he had sunk down behind those rocks and at that very moment was just cowering there, waiting for me to go away.

I was not going to go away. I was not really sure how I was going to do it at that close range, but I was going to stalk up to that rock fence in the woods, stand up, and there he would be, on the other side, point blank, the biggest deer ever seen on the deer pasture. What was the etiquette for such an occasion, for such a stalk? How did one kill a deer at such close range? With a Bowie knife? Would it be unfair not to let him spring up and run twenty yards or so? Was it hard to get the scope on a running deer that is crashing through the brush only twenty yards away? Would it even be sportsmanlike to risk such a shot at a difficult, moving target? What if I hit him in the leg, the shoulder, or, God forbid, the stomach? What if I missed? But if I didn't let him run—if I surprised him—would I actually shoot him from three or four yards away? Was that fair, either?

Needless to say, that was the last I ever saw of that deer. Still not sure of my plans, I sank to my own knees on the other side of the rock fence and began creeping towards it, very quietly, very slowly. I paused often; my heart was hammering. I knew he was just on the other side of the fence, right where I had seen him go down. I was the picture of stealth. I was silent, invisible. It was the most perfect stalk ever made. Even as I reached the fence and then quickly rose up over it, steeling myself for his startled reaction—even then I am not sure what I had in mind doing. Tackling him, I suppose, or wrestling him 'til he said uncle, I don't know.

Only he wasn't there. I couldn't believe it. It was more than embarrassing; it was devastating. It was impossible to look at the spot without feeling the burning realization that the entire time I had been crawling slowly and on my belly across the ground, that during the entire stalk, he had been long gone, and that I had been sneaking up on an empty patch of Gillespie County. That I had pounced on an empty piece of Hill Country.

I walked up the rock ridge; I walked down it. I looked everywhere, as if I might have just missed him, overlooked him, and he was not gone at all but still on the mountain, right under my gaze, as a set of keys or a pair of scissors are in your desk at work when you really need them, and you rummage back and forth over them several times in the clutter without really seeing them, you are looking for them so hard. That is how I surveyed the woods all around me then. As if the biggest deer in the county had not given me the slip but was indeed still there, hiding camouflaged against a patch of deer-colored boulder or something, still waiting for me to leave.

I left, all right. I was sick.

Also, I never saw him again.

And I never hunted that area again, either.

I've got no truck with that deer anymore; he beat me fair and square and soundly; I know my limitations. So now I hunt Buck Hill and the Burned-Off Hill, and I range and roam and see lots of different sights, lots of different deer, and I beat some and get beaten by others.

But I never forget the big deer over on the East Side that I didn't even see enough times to give a name to. The first deer I ever tried to hunt specifically, in Gillespie County, in the Texas Hill Country. The first deer that ever beat me, in Gillespie County, in the Texas Hill Country.

9
Progeny

I'm a jeep man.

The deer pasture is a jeep place.

What's the worst trouble you've ever been in?" Cousin Randy asked.

"I think this is it," I said. We were both sitting clear of the jeep. It was on its side; the dust was still hanging thick, dry, and alkali-like, limey, and the wheels were still spinning. The engine was, muscle of tiny tough muscles, still running, and the radiator was making an angry hissing noise.

But that's the funny thing about the deer pasture. You are kind of happy, sort of, even when you're in the worst trouble you've ever been in in your life—the one time when you realize that this is probably where your father is actually going to make good on the always-before-presumed-joking half-threat of childhood to "break your arm off and beat you over the head with it." (Said thoughout grade school, it was enough to keep us from ringing Miss Hughes's doorbell and then running; said in junior high, it was enough to pull us from a C+ to an A− in mathematics; said in high school, it had us in before one, no matter how important the date.)

But it was not enough to keep us from trying to take a short cut up the back side of Buck Hill that day. We were adults, twenty-five and twenty-eight years old, re-

spectively, and we were terrified. Glad to be in Gillespie County, still, but terrified.

"Maybe we could tell him it was an act of God," said Cousin Randy. Overhead, a hawk wheeled silently. The sky was an electric blue. No one in the Hill Country knew it was November. It was, I thought with some bemusement, as good a place to be in trouble as you could wish for, if you could pick such things.

Do you know how indispensable a jeep is in the Hill Country?

It doesn't matter what year, and though the little four-cylinder Willys Overlands are the best—they're the classics; it's as if the Hill Country was formed for them, and not vice-versa—it really doesn't even matter what model. Toyota, GMC, International Harvester—the Jeep jeep is the best, but even an imitation jeep is better than no jeep.

Trucks do not count. Trucks are a little too big, a little too square and boxy and impersonal. The worst thing about the trucks is that they still have their paint, and are closed

in. I feel trapped in a truck compared to a jeep. In a jeep, I
feel free.

If you do have a truck instead of a jeep, and the truck
doesn't have any paint left, that makes it a little better, but
it still does not make it as good as the jeep. With the jeep,
with the doors and top off, if you want, you can climb rock
faces or back down granite washes in low gear, and it's like
mountain climbing and rappelling. You can cross little
stony streams, and the rocks will skitter out from under the
tires if you cross slowly enough and do it just right, and it is
a personal thing, like the clatter of horses' hooves crossing
a shallow ford.

The Old First Jeep is gone. Randy and I never knew
it. We have one picture of it, staring goggle-eyed and sul-
lenly from back in the depths of the barn. It was before our
time. No one will tell us why it is no longer with us, which
is quite the puzzlement—it is very odd for a jeep to just
stop and no longer be running. (My father grows especially
uncomfortable when we raise the question; was he close to
the jeep? Did he have a hand in its demise? Forget to check
the oil one morning, and throw a rod? Discharge a bullet
through the gas tank? No one is telling.)

Howard still has a jeep, a tiny jeep, a pre-WW jeep,
but he never starts it, never drives it. It sits in back of his
house, and he stores things in it—bridles, saddles, oats.
Howard still uses a cow pony to get around on, down at the
deer pasture. He says the Jeep bounces too much, rides too
stiff, and is too rough on his kidneys, his liver, his spleen,
and his "consumption."

Howard is used to horses. When he has to go into
town, he has a little shell of a Volkswagen Beetle sitting
over four sometimes-inflated tires. There are no wind-
shield wipers, but that is no matter, for there is no wind-
shield, either. Time and rodents and the Hill Country win-

ters have just sort of consumed what were once seats in the little bug, so now there is nothing, not even the rusty steel spring-frames, and to see over the steering wheel he sits on a soap box. The bug used to be purple, and if you are ever in Johnson City on one of those rare occasions when Howard does need something from civilization, you will recognize the car, and it is a good one, and true.

So Howard's jeep isn't the jeep we use, either. The jeep we use now is a sort of a jeep-truck, such as you used to see on "The Waltons." The best of both worlds, really: small, like a jeep, with four-wheel drive and a jeep's heart, but also with a bed behind the cab for hauling lumber, deer, groceries. This is the jeep Cousin Randy and I have rattled around all over the deer pasture in. This is the jeep my father paints anew, shiny grey and polished black, after each hunt and enters in an antique car show every now and then. It is quite classy, with two five-gallon drums of gas holstered on either side of the cab, and it still has the original radio. This is the jeep that Cousin Randy and I stared upon mournfully. It looked naked lying on its side.

"No," I said slowly, "I do not think he will buy the act of God excuse again."

There had already been too many acts of God. Even for a place like the deer pasture.

Sometimes really crazy things happen at the deer pasture. Odd things. Things that you would guess to have, say, a one-in-a-million chance of happening. Sometimes you get six or seven such things to happen to you in a single day, down there, so that they no longer seem miraculous, but rather typical, even expected.

"There's a buck," Randy said quietly. "He's moving through those boulders across the creek, coming towards us."

I saw the deer he was talking about. He was sort of

sneaking down the hill, with his tail tucked and his head sort of cast down, like a dog tracking a scent, as bucks sometimes do when they are following a doe. Either that or his rack was too heavy for him to hold his head up the way bucks usually do. It was quite the big rack.

Or it could have been that the old deer was senile. The wheels were still spinning; the radiator was still hissing. Cousin Randy and I were sitting square in the middle of nothing, perched atop two ledges above the creek, looking down at our fiasco. Anybody and everything in Gillespie County could have seen us.

Perhaps the deer was blind, I thought.

Our guns were still in the gun rack. Upended, but still in the rack.

Bass's Rule of the Deer Pasture No. 2: Always strap any rifles and shotguns into the gun rack. (Bass's Rule No. 1: Never allow a loaded gun in the jeep).

Cousin Randy and I looked at each other at the same time.

Cousin Randy and I are close, but not that close.

I got to the jeep first; Cousin Randy was a close but very definite second. He sighed, but then submitted to my own excitement and began to hyperexcite himself, whispering small, useless bits of encouragement, such as "Take your time" and "Stay calm." I dropped a bullet in the dust, trying to hurry it into the chamber, and bumped heads with Randy as we both bent quickly down to retrieve it.

It was getting embarrassing; the deer was still coming, getting closer, so close that I realized it was not impossible that he might soon be too close, too close to shoot, too close to find in the scope, before I got the bullet in. It was like being charged in slow motion.

I got the bullet in; I slid the bolt home.

I crouched down, braced the barrel against the boulder for support, found it not to my liking, and searched for and got a better brace against a little oak.

Bass's Rule of the Deer Pasture No. 3: Bracing a rifle against a support for a better shot is not unmanly. Shooting a deer in the leg or in the stomach or some other place that causes it much pain and confusion and fright and suffering is unmanly.

The deer was in the creek bottom. I fired. He dropped. Cousin Randy and I grinned, we whooped, even. It was a beautiful day, suddenly, even more so than before. The sky was still blue, and the sun continued to stream down. I looked up, grinning, just feeling good, sort of drunk on beauty, and saw the hawk flying off, his wings beating hard, carrying him fast and away to more Hill Country silence. We got up and began working our way down our bank to where the monster lay with his legs folded under him and head out. It was a beautiful rack. His muzzle was grey, but he was not senile; his neck was as thick as a ham. He had been doe-crazy.

"It happens to the best of us," said Cousin Randy. We admired the deer for a while. It was easily the biggest deer that either of us had ever seen killed on the deer pasture. We admired it so much that we did not see or hear my father, who had been up in the boulders, too, stalking the deer I had just shot, come walking down.

My father is a very quiet walker.

"You shot my deer," he said. "I had to sit up in the rocks and watch as you shot my deer."

"Oops," I said. It was all I could think of.

Also, I was using his gun. That was something else I forgot to tell you: I had asked to borrow one of his that morning, since mine wasn't shooting straight.

"You shot my deer, with my gun," he said.

I could tell Cousin Randy was starting to be awful glad

it was me and not he who had gotten to the rifles first after
all. It even looked like he was having to bite his lip to keep
from grinning. I remember wondering, somewhat abstrac-
tedly, what my father's reaction would be if Randy was
actually to laugh out loud.

Only he, my father, didn't seem really mad. A little
surprised, yes, a little puzzled, but also, oh, I don't
know—amused? I swear it could even be mistaken for
trace-proudness.

Also, he was looking at the jeep.

The radiator had stopped hissing, but still it kind of
drew our attention, sitting there on its side in the dry
creek. It looked spectacularly out of place; it looked like a
tennis shoe plopped down on an exquisitely set hundred-
dollar-a-plate dinner table.

Maybe he would think it was an act of God.

He was incredulous. He was astounded. He was agog.
Like a man in a trance, he left the deer, ignored the deer,
and wandered over to where the jeep lay, unbroken but in-
operable, temporarily out of order. Sidelined.

"How did you do that?" he asked. He had set his rifle down and was walking around the jeep slowly, examining it like a man studying a race horse. He felt the bumper, ran his hand over the fender. Thumped the headlight. He looked up the hill, where we had first started the roll. Up at the bare old monstrous live oak root that had sidetracked our tires and started our tumble. It was very still; there was not even a breeze. Not even a little one. I pointed up the hill to the tree. To the Old Moss Tree. I sort of mumbled. "I, um, kind of, um. . . ."

He was very interested; he was intensely curious. He watched me as I mumbled. I did not think I could ever remember him being so fascinated.

"Did anyone tell you?" he asked. He looked at me, then at Cousin Randy, then back at me. "No, you don't know, of course not." He started walking around the jeep, still dumbfounded.

"This is the exact place, the exact same position the Old First Jeep was in when I rolled it twenty years ago," he said, and when he looked up, he was kind of grinning a little—an amazed grin. "This is the very same spot, to the inch. Only I totaled the jeep I rolled; the engine fell out and rolled into the creek, and a big buck didn't come walking down out of the rocks after I did it.'

There was no doubt about it, he was looking at me with a kind of a proud grin, the kind of grin that you have to be a guy to feel, and you have to have it grinned at you by your father. It was the kind of grin that makes you feel awful good.

We field-dressed the deer, hung him up in a tree, hiked back to camp, and got in about dark, just as pots were clanging in the kitchen. We could see little yellow squares of warm light in the cabin as we crested Camp Hill. We got everyone excited about the big deer and borrowed Howard's bug and somehow all crowded into it, sitting cross-legged on the floor like gypsies, and bounced over rocks and up canyons and through the Hill Country night and back down to the creek and righted the jeep. Started it up, marveled at the deer, put it in the back, and drove back to camp. Had a not-too-latish supper of biscuits and steak fingers and red wine. Took the jeep into Fredericksburg at lunch the next day and had the radiator patched for thirty-five dollars.

Bass's Rule of the Deer Pasture No. 4: No yelling at another member of one's family is allowed while in camp. Absolutely none. No matter what.

It's not such a hard rule. I rather enjoy it.

IO
The Storyteller

I don't want you to get the idea that all we do at the deer pasture is sit around by the campfire at night and tell stories, but sometimes we do, and when we do, they are usually good ones. My father is the champion; far and away, he tells the best. This is one of my favorites; I heard it on my first hunt.

". . . and sure enough, there is a man lying out there, right smack dab in the middle of the yard. Dogs are barking and howling, and all the neighbors are turning on their porch lights and looking out their windows. Just as Ken is getting out of the car, this hobo raises his arms straight up in the air like a zombie coming out of a casket, only much faster, and then he jumps up off the lawn and starts waltzing across the grass, tearing off articles of clothing. He whirls over to the petunias and pulls his windbreaker off before dashing over to the mailbox and stuffing his shirt into it. Ken starts after him, and he runs around to the back of the house. They're making lap after lap around the house, Ken gaining on him little by little, and each time the thug runs around the front yard, he kicks off a shoe or a sock or unbuckles his belt. And all this time he is just screaming and yelling like he was on fire. Finally Ken gets really close to him, so the hobo decides he'd better stop running in circles around the house and get away while he can. He takes off down the street, clad only in his underwear, singing at the top of his lungs and cackling like a hyena. Ken never did find out who it was."

Having just finished the story, my father stood up and tossed another stick of wood on the fire, sending a kaleidoscope of red and yellow sparks some twenty or thirty feet into the cold, dark night sky. The sparks hung suspended for a moment, blending in with the Hill Country stars, and then fell back to the ground, disappearing before they landed.

Cousin Randy ducked into the cabin for a moment and came back out with a bag of toasting-sized marshmallows, which he passed around after opening them and taking out a handful for himself. Everyone sat silent for a while, musing on the story.

"He was pretty weird," Uncle Jimmy finally said.

My father sat back down on the story-telling log and coughed, rubbing his hands together before holding them out so that the palms faced the fire, warming them, looking as if he was trying to ward away some advancing menace. The flames flared up, lighting up everyone's faces, and the orange glow made everyone's eyes seem dark and wet and clear; not like animal eyes, but not like their own eyes, either—at least not what they looked like back in the city.

My father coughed again. "Yeah, he was pretty weird, but I'd have to say that old Hinchie had them all beat when it came to weirdness. He just radiated it, like a toaster oven. You couldn't even get near him without noticing that he was absolutely bizarre."

"He was the one with all the armadillos, wasn't he?" Cousin Randy asked from back in the shadows.

"Yeah, he was the one with all the armadillos," my father said, and moved a little closer to the fire. My father and Uncle Jimmy had gone to school in Austin; Hinchie had been their roommate for one semester, the first.

"He was a Hill Country boy, from Eckert, and he had

all sorts of odd things living with him—skunks, coons, snakes, gators, lion cubs, even a little chimp, but the armadillos were his claim to fame. They used to drive his landlord up the wall, when Hinchie was in school. He was doing metabolism studies on them and used to let them run around the yard like dogs. He had a great time with them; sometimes he'd walk them on a leash, and he even had one trained to hop like a kangaroo—it would rear up on its hind legs and take off down the sidewalk, making maybe five or six feet a hop.

"They were really pretty intelligent. I had always thought of them as, well, reptilian at best, but his little nieces and nephews—he had five of them—just adored the beasts. They used to come over every Sunday afternoon for a tea party. Their mom would drive up in the station wagon after church every Sunday and they'd pile out of the car and run screaming across the yard, hollering for Uncle Hinchie and Jubu, the largest armadillo. The mother would never get out of the car; she was terrified of the place.

"Anyway, these kids always brought along a suitcase full of the latest styles in infants' clothing—their father owned the largest Cadillac dealership in the state—people used to drive clear from Lubbock to Austin just to buy a car from his store—and they would get Hinchie to help them dress the armadillos for the tea party. I often wondered if the father ever dreamed that part of his salary was going towards buying new clothes for his brother's family of armadillos each week.

"They would always dress Jubu in the sailor's suit and give him a sporty little blue cap that had holes cut in it for his pointed ears. Jubu's sidekick—they called her Miss Piggy, and I swear the Muppets got their character from her—was always attired in a fetching gingerbread-colored gingham dress that swept the ground when she walked. The others would wear whatever was new that

week. The armadillos behaved well, and they would all get very quiet while the children were dressing them, making no sounds except for this funny little purring noise like a cat does when it rubs up against your leg. I really believe they liked it.

"Then Hinchie would wheel the wrought-iron table out in the front yard and bring some chairs out, and they'd all go out and sit at the table and just watch the cars drive by while they had their tea party in the middle of Austin, Texas. They had high chairs for the armadillos, and usually sprinkled a few grasshoppers or beetles on their tray along with a candy bar—they loved chocolate bars—while Hinchie and the children sipped tea and nibbled on Girl Scout cookies.

"They must have caused quite a sensation in the town on any given Sunday—a grown man, five kids, and six armadillos all seated around this table, buffet style, out in the middle of this incredibly hot country—Austin never saw a day under 100° in the dead of summer—sipping tea and crunching grasshoppers.

"Jubu was by the far the most refined; they always tucked a large white cloth napkin in his shirt collar, though he rarely spilled, and they got a parasol for Miss Piggy— she was paler than the others and burned easily, so they just strapped it over her tray to shade her from the sun. The armadillos were very polite about the whole thing; they would just sit patiently, looking about with a detached look of amusement on their snouts, occasionally breaking into a crocodile grin when one of the children spilled his tea.

"As soon as the party was over, the kids would take the armadillos' napkins out of their laps and wipe the corners of their mouths ever so daintily before picking them up by their tails, so that they held them upside down, and setting them gently on the ground. The armadillos would then scamper off to their den under the house, snorting and jumping and playing like school children let out at recess.

"The armadillo family was always rooting around in the front yard, digging holes and burrows in search of insects, so they soon had an entire underground network of tunnels and caves that led all across the town. One afternoon the landlord was over at the house checking up on things, Hinchie included. The landlord had this grubby little toy poodle that always messed on the lawn and yapped at sparrows and grasshoppers and occasionally at a small kitten if it was feeling really bold.

"Well, the landlord—I think his name was Jack—Jack

Ripps, that's it—was walking this brute of a dog around the yard, just kind of looking around, when the dog trotted over to one of these mounds in the front yard. Jack got pretty riled when he saw it, and he let go of the leash and got down on all fours, peering down this hole, trying to see what it was. And of course the killer poodle was all blood and guts with his master there right next to him; he was barking and snapping at the air and tearing up the ground with his claws, trying to stick his nose down there too.

"All of a sudden there was this great bronze blur, glinting in the sun, and Jubu came hopping out of that hole like he was launched from an underground trampoline—he just sailed out of the hole and kept going straight up so that at the peak of his jump he was well above Jack's crouching eye level. The big armadillo came down right on top of the poodle, and before Jack could even be sure that he had seen it, he had dragged the dog back down into that hole. There was this horrible snarling and howling and then a couple of whimpers, and then all was quiet. Someone down the street was mowing their lawn, and Jack could taste the smell of fresh-cut grass. Stunned, he looked around the yard dumbly and thought to himself that his own yard needed mowing.

"So Hinchie had to move. He couldn't find anyplace that would take him in; people distrusted bachelors more back then than they do now, and besides, almost everyone had seen him walk-hopping his armadillos to school. He finally ended up sleeping on a cot in his office at the school— he was a graduate assistant there, but already had seven or eight degrees from schools all over the country—and took his showers down at the Y.M.C.A. He used to throw all his laundry into this big burlap bag he kept in one corner of the office and take it in to the washateria every now and then. And of course the armadillo had the run of the place, curling up under the typewriter, nesting in the trash can, and so on.

"Anyway, one day Jubu disappeared. Hinchie figured he had gotten out while he was in class or something and didn't worry about it too much; he was almost through with the study anyway. What he didn't know was that Jubu hadn't left the room but was instead living in the dirty clothes bag. He found out a month later.

"He had been up real late the night before, working up a herpetology midterm, so he wasn't too quick on his feet and never even noticed when he dumped all the clothes— whites and colors together—into the washing machine. He threw a bucket of soap in and put a quarter in the slot and then he went over and sat against the wall and napped while all the housewives dried their hair or wrote letters or did needlepoint. The whole time he kept hearing this cla-dang, cla-dang noise, like a pair of heavy tennis shoes going around in the dryer, and he figured that's what it was.

"As soon as the washer went into the spin-dry cycle, Jubu made his escape. The washer lid popped open, and he poked his long, pointed nose out and peeked around at all the housewives and schoolteachers. All covered with suds, he then scrambled out onto the top of the washer, took what looked to be a deep breath, and hurled himself out away from the washer and landed heavily on the floor, spraying everyone with dirty water. Shaking himself like a wet dog, he paused and looked around the small room, stunned from his jump.

"The tallest lady—a librarian—screamed, and Jubu snapped out of his reverie, and like some great Tide-blue dinosaur, he sneezed and started ambling towards her, his weak eyes squinting as he made his way towards what he thought was an oak tree. The would-be oak screamed again and jumped up onto the nearest dryer, terrifying Jubu no end. He, too, jumped straight up into the air and made another little sneezing sound which all the other ladies misinterpreted as a sort of anger-snort, and they all started screaming and stampeded for the only door, but he whirled around and cut them off at the Coke machine, which was between them and the door.

"All this time Hinchie was chasing after him, trying to grab his slippery tail. Finally he caught up with him and grabbed his tail and hoisted him up into the air like a proud fisherman with a trophy catch, and all the ladies screamed again. He smiled his best Eddie Haskell smile at them and walked over to the dryer, turned the dial to warm, and placed the miscreant Jubu in there along with all the other clothes as if he were nothing more than another pair of pants.

"Rubbing his chin thoughtfully, he shook his head and as an afterthought he turned the dial back to lukewarm and put the dime in before returning to his seat and picking up a paperback, looking up only occasionally to see Jubu running around the cylinder like a hamster on a treadmill, a wild look in his eyes, tail banging against the glass window every now and then."

My father yawned and stood up, stretching, and then yawned again. "Look, there goes a shooting star," he said, pointing directly above us, and a few of us looked in time to catch the tail end of it.

"What happened to Jubu?" Cousin Randy asked, still looking up at the sky as if he expected the falling star to reappear and head back the other way so that he can see it this time.

"Huh?" my father said, turning around to look at him.

"Jubu—whatever happened to him?" Randy repeated.

"Oh, Jubu," my father said. "Hinchie took him home along with the clean clothes."

"Was he all right?" Grandaddy asked, amazed.

"I don't know—guess so," my father said. He looked back up at the stars.

"I'm going to hit the hay—I'll see y'all before the sun comes up," he said, and walked off towards the bunkhouse.

The deer are secondary, they really are.

II
Bass's Wonder Biscuits

SHALL I tell you of the wonderment of Bass's Hill Country Biscuits? Have you been really good?

No one can fix them except Uncle Jimmy. I swear that's the Gospel truth. He's given us the recipe, we've all tried, back at home, for Fourth of July picnics, lazy Saturday morning breakfasts, football games, Monday night football games, and they don't work. Oh, they come out all right, usually; I mean, they rise and everything, but the difference is like . . . oh . . . you know those rolls you buy twelve-to-a-pack, the old white factory kind that are molded as one in the package, so that you have to tear them as if along a dotted line, to separate them? The kind you sometimes get with your order at a fast-food chicken-order place? That's what Bass's Hill Country Biscuits taste like if you try to fix them anywhere else but the deer pasture. But I'll give you the recipe anyway:

2 lbs boned venison (ham, shoulder)
2 6-oz cans tomato paste
6 oz hot water (add more if needed)
¾ cup wine vinegar
1¼ cups unsweetened pineapple juice
¾ cup brown sugar
3 tbsp lemon juice
½ tsp each black pepper, salt, chili powder, dry mustard
1 clove garlic, minced
4 cups biscuit mix
1⅓ cup nonfat milk

Cut venison into 1½-inch cubes. In kettle, combine all ingredients but biscuit mix and milk. Stir, cover. Bring to boil, reduce heat to simmer, and cook 1 hour or more. Long, slow cooking is best. Shred meat with fork. Heat oven to 450°. Beat biscuit mix and milk together. Roll out dough ¼ to ½ inch thick. Cut into 24 circles. Spoon meat onto one circle, top with another, and pinch edges together. Bake on greased cookie sheet 8–10 minutes, until brown. Serves six normal people, five if they have been deer hunting.

The second or third night in camp, Uncle Jimmy usually makes a couple hundred or so. We keep them in a big greasy paper sack in the refrigerator. In the mornings, all dressed up and ready to go, hunting pants on, heavy shell-jackets on, rifles slung over our shoulders, binoculars around our necks, hiking boots on, we'll reach in the bag, reach into the bottom, pawlike, and grab a couple and put them in our coat pocket for a snack. I usually eat mine before I am halfway up Camp Hill. They're super energy; each biscuit has about three hundred calories and fifteen grams of protein. It's all there—vitamins A, C, B1, B2, B6, B12, niacin, calcium, iron, phosphorous, magnesium, zinc, copper—the deer don't have a chance.

In dominoes and cards we sometimes use the biscuits for poker chips.

It is a sad moment, the last day of camp, when the last biscuit is eaten.

They never taste the same anywhere else.

12
Spring

AND in April the deer pasture is spring busted loose. Even
the rusted old farm parts up in the high places seem to
shout it. Yes, it's a cliché to say things "shout" spring's arrival, but they do; you can see them rusting up there in the
meadows, wise from suffering, see them up there in the
meadows before you nose on off down into the creek canyons and cactus knob-hills and slickrock gullies filled with
house-sized rounded boulders as if some druid of a giant
had, called off to some important place in a hurry, swept
all his many nonvaluable but very beautiful precious play-
pretties—boulders, mostly, but also logs and cacti and
grapes and Spanish moss and live oaks big enough down
along the creeks and with enough moss and shady enough
to break your heart—it's as if he hurriedly swept all these
things down out of the flat, giving meadows and with his
giant hands dropped them into those deep troughs and
basins and ravines and arroyos and then went off to his important place and forgot them.

All I can say is, it must have been one hell of an important place.

Driving by on the county roads, through the area they
call the Devil's Backbone, you get stirring views, pano-
ramas, vistas, sweep and grandeur—the whole thing—but
then, up into the Hill Country proper, where people like
Howard live and raise goats and sheep and turkeys and the
grass is nibbled down close and the rocks are flat and
the sun hot and not quite as far away as it was down in the

lowlands—up there, you can drive past these sometimes little, sometimes big meadows and never dream that you're up on a shelf of geologic time, a short-circuit in time and history, and that just a mile or two on over to the west (always, it seems, always to the west), down that chalky white limestone-gravel road, through those monstrously tough little cedar jungles, and across the tha-dumptha-dump of a cattle guard, lies the basin of druid-toy playthings, and we are forced to marvel once again at what made Grandaddy turn in where he did, when he did, that dry and dusty lazy Hill Country summer day forty-nine years ago.

But springs are the loveliest. Springs are when we bring the girls.

The "girls" include Grandma; Mom; Janie, Howard's daughter, who is sixty and is as close to being tough-as-nails as anyone in this world can be; Aunt Lee; and this last spring, Lory. Randy's eyes widened perceptibly when I showed up with her; you could see the alarm in them, but I quieted him with a subtle wave of my hand—a sort of reassuring, calm, side-to-side "it's okay, it's not what it seems" gesture. But he still seemed rattled; he still seemed unconvinced. Shaken, almost.

In Bass history, bringing a girl to the deer pasture is like taking her to a jewelry store to look at some rings.

Things happen. Bad things, from my and Cousin Randy's points of view. So "it's okay" is the little hand signal I gave Randy when we got out of the car. But you could tell he wasn't convinced. You could tell he was worried.

The deer pasture is where Dad brought Mom one spring about twenty-seven years ago. He didn't ask her there, but that is where he decided he would eventually ask her somewhere. And four years before that, it's the place where Uncle Jimmy brought Aunt Lee, who was not yet Aunt Lee but who after that day said she would be.

Oh, the deer pasture's a dangerous, dangerous place to bring a girl, to bring a pretty girl, especially in the spring.

Lory busied herself talking with the other women, excited, a set-free-after-a-long-drive excitement, an arrived-at-a-destination sort of excitement; they all had it. So did we, for that matter, the guys. We kind of split up, went down and checked the water pump, grinning, asking each other how our respective drives in had been. Cousin Randy seemed relieved that I had paired off away from Lory right from the start, to be with the guys.

The sun felt good, walking down to the water pump. The bluebonnets and crimson of the Indian paintbrushes brushed up against our ankles. We puttered around with the pump, got it humming, got it making its high little winding sounds. A little green frog, the size of a child's matchbox toy, *Rana catesbeiana*, watched us from a lily pad. There was a lot of algal bloom in the creek. It was a sunny spring. I looked down the creek and then up at all the jumble of rock and boulder and cactus and loneliness and beauty over on the East Side, and I felt good, felt like running around or doing some jumping jacks or push-ups. I turned and looked back up towards the cabin and saw Lory—she was looking at me—and we grinned at each other, kept looking at each other. Then I saw that Randy was watching me with a look of utter incredulity, and I looked quickly away, but every now and then I would sneak a look back up the hill at Lory, and she would be watching me, smiling, and I would feel real funny inside, real funny.

"Let's go look for armadillos," Randy said, "like we do every year," and there was so much I wanted to show Lory, so much I wanted her to see, so much I wanted to share, and we were only going to be there for the weekend. But you can't turn down your cousin, whom you don't see but four times every year, Christmas, Thanksgiving, the deer hunt, and the spring trip—you can't tell him that you don't have time to go look for armadillos with him. Not when it's something you've done every spring. Not when it's something that only takes a couple of hours. Even if you would rather more than anything else be spending those two hours, those first two hours upon your arrival, with your girl friend. Who is really a little more than a girl friend, else you would not have brought her here in the first place.

Cousin Randy and I saw our first armadillo about one hundred and fifty yards out of camp, up the first branch off of Camp Creek. He—the armadillo, not Cousin Randy—

was snuffling around in a meadow with his head down, really rooting, else he'd probably have heard us.

"God, I love the spring," Cousin Randy whispered. Armadillos are legally blind, were armadillos to have legislation on such things, but they have very big ears, like radar dishes, to pick up the sounds of little bugs and things pattering around in the leaves. Our armadillo had his head down, though, and was making labored, snorting, sniffing sounds as he ripped the meadow earth with his claws, pointed his snout down into his digs, and began furrowing. Stalking the ever-elusive carabinid beetle. In quest of aphids. Blissfully ignorant of our presence, thinking only one primitive thought: food, food, food. Cousin Randy and I watched him root. It was sort of a tradition.

I guess by now you are beginning to suspect, beginning to realize, that that's what the deer pasture is all about; that that's why we, and so many other thousands of hunters, get so worked up about it each November. It's sort of a constant in the year; it's a yardstick, the one thing that doesn't change, a measuring point, a high-water mark, but it's more. It's an anchor. Cousin Randy and I watched armadillos last year, and now we were watching them this year, just as it was a sure thing that we would watch them again next year. If I didn't get married and move to Washington, D.C., and have a baby, quadruplets even, between now and then. If I stayed single and free and wild and worthwhile. Unattached. If I kept things as they were—frozen, constant.

"You won't get married and move to Washington, D.C., and have Responsibilities this time next year, will you?" Randy asked worriedly. He was watching the armadillo still, speaking in a low tone still, but you could tell he was really upset. Fretting, he was. It was as if it was his own bachelorhood that was being threatened.

Cousin Randy's twenty-ninth birthday was last October. To celebrate, he and I flew out to Denver on one of those excursion fares and had dinner. We went on a Saturday afternoon. Just a whim, just a splurge. We were back Sunday afternoon. Foolish, really, but it helped keep us young.

No, I started to tell him, don't worry, everything's okay. I really did start to tell him that, but just then the armadillo looked up and caught us; we had to freeze and watch him watch us, rearing up on his hind legs like a shelled prairie dog, squinting, his snout shaking and quivering furiously as he scowled in our direction, ears cupped out and flared perpendicular so as to pick up even the slightest sounds of our breathing or of our eyelids closing. He watched, squinted intently, and then, having made his decision, dropped to all fours, turned broadside to us, and began to pretend to be casting around for more bugs and things, but he was onto us, you could tell, for he was moving away from us. We kind of started to slink towards him, on tip-toes, as quiet as we could, but of course if he could hear our breathing then he could certainly hear our muted but still heavy, collective three-hundred and seventy-five pounds' worth of footsteps—we weighed one hundred and seventy-five pounds each (a grasshopper, twelve grams)—and he dropped the pretense and began waddling towards some trees, in a straight line now, no sidling or pretense of wandering about it now. Too dignified to run, yet, but too frightened to ignore us. We broke and ran for him. He made his little sneezing sound of alarm, leapt straight up and high into the air, as if shocked by the ground, and bolted.

If you have never seen an armadillo bolt, you need to set down whatever it is you are doing right now, mark the place in the book with a scrap of Kleenex or something, go out to your garage, get in your car, and begin driving for the Texas Hill Country. If you are in some faraway place

like Philadelphia or Mount Pleasant, Michigan, bring a camera so that your friends back home will believe it. Stop at any old meadow you come to once you're inside Gillespie County. Crouch behind a cedar. Wait. Listen. You will hear him before you see him, hear him come snuffling through the grass and leaves making a noise like some rain-dance shuffle-step known only to armadillos and shamans: rustle, rustle, pause-pause; rustle, rustle. Pause.

Do wrong, snap his picture during the pause instead of the rustle, when his wizened little pointed-snout whiskered face is straight up in the air, sniffing and listening for enemies, and he'll snort, leap, and run, and you can't catch him. Because he runs fast, a sort of a scamper only much faster—it is like a frantic, over-sprung wind-up toy. And also, because he dodges things. Trees, rocks—usually. Armadillos are near-sighted, and occasionally they cut to the right side at the last instant, but sometimes their shells hinder their agility, and they run into things instead of around them. But it is no matter; their shells are hard, protective, and they merely bounce off at a tangent and keep running in a new direction until they hit another obstacle and take off in another direction.

So take his picture. Snap it when he's rustling, though, rooting for bugs, and not when he's pausing. Wave it a-round at office parties, show it to your friends, relatives, and other acquaintances.

They will be agog.

There was not much to do after Cousin Randy's and my armadillo bolted except chase it. I was a little out of shape from my desk job and still had on tennis shoes, not hiking boots, and stiff jeans, not walking shorts, but that, too, was tradition, the chasing of the first armadillo we saw, and he had started it anyway, bolting as he had. It was like a challenge, so Cousin Randy and I sprinted after him. There was no difference at all in the way we sprinted after this armadillo and the way we had sprinted after armadillos in the spring when we were fourteen and growing like weeds and not even thinking about it.

It's medicine, yes, and this may be simplistic and granola-bars-and-lotus-position philosophy, but I think, I really do, that people from all walks of life would be a lot better, a lot less tense, if only even every now and then they could be walking down a creek or through the woods or across a meadow and suddenly startle an armadillo and give wild chase. It might make the Gillespie County arma-dillo population a little more tense, a little more wary, but I am convinced it would do wonders for the human segment.

Also, I guess I could tell you that you'll never catch one, that they're too fast, that in thirteen years Cousin Randy and I have never caught even one, but that might spoil it for you, might discourage you before you start, so I'll just tell you this: we didn't catch this particular armadillo.

"Would Lory chase an armadillo with you if y'all were out walking and saw one?" Cousin Randy asked. We were pulling Camp Hill, headed back, breathing hard from the

chase. It was a good question. "I mean, would she if you asked her? If you tore out after one, would she think it was fun and follow?"

It was a real good question.

She's never even seen an armadillo.

Cousin Randy saw me pondering the question and smirked. Oh, he was so smart.

"She might," I said defensively, quickly, when I saw the smirk. "I don't know that she wouldn't."

That night, we all got together around the fire. The night was nice, kind of warm, and Dad had fixed steaks for everyone, real big steaks, steaks as big as license plates and two inches high. Cousin Randy and Lory and I each had a beer; we were listening to stories, none of them new, and it was good. Mom had a bouquet of bluebonnets that Dad had picked for her earlier in the day—fifty-one years, my tough old father, and he did that; surely the deer pasture is a magical place to make you do that—and I was holding Lory in front of me, watching the fire. She was talking to Randy and laughing; we were all pretty happy and full, and no one was sick, and I felt great, as great as I could ever remember feeling, and for no reason at all, really, which may have actually been the reason.

Oh, well, there could have been one small reason, I guess, just a little something that happened earlier in the day.

For a ring, I gave her a pop-top from a can of Lone Star.

13
Werner

DRIVING through Texas deer hunting country, whether it is deer season or not, you have to wave at any passing cars or trucks. It's mandatory; not waving is not an option. If you are mad at the world or have an ulcer, you don't have to smile, but you must wave.

But no one has ulcers. Not in Texas deer hunting country.

Come to think of it, no one is ever mad at the world there, either.

Take, for instance, Werner Schnappauf. I have seen Werner hit his thumb with a hammer and frown, perplexed, and then go back to work. That is all. No physical violence, no temper tantrum, no abusive language. It is over and done with. He has made a mistake, but the pain is gone; he returns to his chore, his work.

You'd be in a bad way without work in the Texas Hill Country. A lot of you may have the impression of, and sometimes you may even have seen little vignettes of the old country man on the porch, slat-floor boards askew, hound lying in the dust with chin tucked between front paws, sunset, overgrown weeds in the back choking a single spindly peach tree, maybe . . . cowbells, perhaps, down on the creek, as evening comes in. No sir. The peach trees don't make it; they'd be eaten by the goats or baked by the sun or crushed in an ice storm. There may be dogs, but they chase sheep, nip at their fat, muttonous heels with canine, barely restrained, impatient fury, furious at the

dumbness of the animals, and there may even be a floor-
board or two askew on the front porch, but there sure as
fire'll not be an old man in the country sitting out on them
watching the sun go down. No, sir, you won't ever catch
him doing that.

They have rocking chairs in the Texas Hill Country,
but I swear no one ever uses them.

The way I met Mr. Schnappauf was when the jeep
needed a new starter. I didn't know that it needed a new
starter, I just knew it wouldn't start. My father and Cousin
Randy and I had been having to push the jeep up to the top
of the road outside camp and then roll-start it down in
second gear. I do not remember how the arrangements
were arrived at, but Cousin Randy steered while my father
and I pushed. It was my father's and my idea to take the
jeep into Fredericksburg on the off chance that we might
find someone who not only knew enough about 1974 Willys
cabbed jeeps to repair them but also was not a deer hunter.

We got lucky.

He raised the hood and looked at it before he said he could fix it. I liked that.

"Ya," he said, and it's corny, it's cliché, but dadgummit, the best things in life are. I watched closely to make sure I wasn't imagining it, just making it up because that was what I wanted to see, but no, sure enough, there it was, his eyes were twinkling, corny or not. You could tell he knew he was fixing to do an awfully good thing.

It is sad that at this point in my life I had been away from Texas deer hunting country so long that I then thought that doing good was corny.

"I bet you vant it back running as soon as possible, ya?" he asked.

He had a tight, clipped, happy, wonderful accent. It was the accent of a craftsman, of a do-gooder. It was a corny accent. His eyes twinkled some more as he watched us. "I vill get to vork on it right avay," he said, and there his eyes went, doing that thing again, that thing that I thought at first I was imagining because it was what I so wanted to see.

He could have ordered a new starter from Austin and had it in by the next day, perhaps, or at the latest the day after that, but instead what he did, taking his time, moving around so casually that we forgot we were in a hurry, was to pull the starter out (he put each little nut and bolt in a little brown paper sack to keep from losing one—I liked that, too) and then he disassembled it, the starter, into a myriad of vulnerable and unattached-looking parts, and then he got his soldering iron and did some messing around on one of the parts, grinning as he did it.

He enjoyed fixing things.

He had, he told us, come over here, to Fredericksburg, from Germany fifty years ago last summer and had been running this shop on the little creek on West Travis Street ever since. He was seventy-five. He had just gotten back from Germany; he'd gone over there to visit his relatives who were still living. It seemed an awful long way from the hot little radiator-generator-alternator auto electric shop on the little creek in Fredericksburg, Texas. He was his only employee.

We talked about deer, too, as he worked; he asked us questions that told us he knew about them. He told us that he had been seeing them eating more acorns this year. He said this, and suddenly it became very easy to imagine this quiet man with the accent from the Old Country sitting up on a hill somewhere watching deer feed in the middle of the day while taking his lunch break, of course, in between jeeps and tractors. What would a man like Mr. Schnappauf eat for lunch? He was a bachelor. A tunafish sandwich and an apple and a can of beer? Potato chips and a carton of milk? A sausage and biscuit left over from breakfast? A bubbly-pop fizz soda?

There was a rocking chair on the porch of his house, which was right next to the garage. I had to ask him. "Mr. Schnappauf, do you ever sit in that rocker?" It was an out of the blue question, quick and certain, and would have surprised another—was I interested in buying it?—but it didn't surprise him.

"Oh, naw," he said, smiling, grinning, his eyes doing that thing again. And then he sort of blushed and looked down at the ground, at the soil of Gillespie County, and grinned wider, as if I had discovered some square little secret about himself, frou frou, to be sure, but a secret nonetheless, a secret which was now to be shared. And since shared secrets by nature make the sharers closer, I grinned, too, closer to this man I'd just met, and we left, left the auto yard of neatly arranged quasi-orchard-rowed tractors and trucks, farm cars and station wagons, lawn mowers and water pumps, and for a long time I imagined I could hear so clearly as if he had just uttered it the happy echo, "Oh, naw," wherever I turned, wherever I walked, wherever I traipsed.

In camp that night, I was the happiest I'd been yet on the trip, without really being able to define it. It was a new-start kind of happy. A Texas Hill Country deer hunting sort of happy. A third day in deer camp happy.

14
Sputnik's Owner

BEFORE he died, Mr. Edgar Gold, Sputnik's owner, could do all sorts of neat things. He could field dress a deer and tie him up so you could carry it in its skin. He had a way of cutting the skin from the hams so he could then somehow loop the legs around a stick so you could carry it in a fireman's drag. Cousin Randy and I never saw him do it. Dad and Uncle Jimmy and Grandaddy did though, lots of times, but when we ask them about it, their faces grow kind of funny and they get kind of vague as they try to explain, and they are not really sure either; it is just one of those things they never learned from him before he died.

Mr. Edgar Gold could do this, too: bring an armadillo to within spitting distance just by gathering up a handful of pebbles and skittering them across the dry leaves so that they sounded like little bugs and beetles, skittering them just out of the old bugger's near-sighted reach, always leading him on. I had read about it being done, but he was the first one I ever saw who could actually do it. It took a lot of patience.

He could gobble like a wild turkey.

He loved to fish for bream in the big pond below the waterfall a little ways up Camp Creek.

The second most amazing thing to us about Mr. Edgar Gold was that he was born on November 16, which used to be the opening day of deer season. Back when he still hunted, I was way too young to go on the hunts, but I remember nonetheless being very impressed by that fact and another one: he would always go out on his birthday and shoot a deer. I was impressed that the old man, living alone, was able to get by on one deer a year, and by the romance of his getting up early on his birthday and going out and hunting, on the opening day of deer season, the most exciting and prettiest day of the year in the Texas Hill Country. I was also impressed by the fact that with seeming aplomb and nonchalance he always got one. Ho-hum, another year, another deer. Almost like it was a duty. He was good and knew where all the deer were. I liked that. He noticed things.

Mr. Edgar Gold's family was one of the first in Gillespie County; they were pioneers down there, back in Indian times, and he had lots of wonderful and perfect arrowheads on shelves all around his cabin. He said they were Comanches; I don't know if they were or not. It sounded too good to risk looking in a book and finding out it was not so. For a fact, he could find an arrowhead on command, and tell you what kind of game it had been used for: squirrel, coon, bird, deer, bear. He would always analyze the ones I found, the ones I came running up to him with, still a child, and remark, tersely, always, the damning word: "Scraper."

Anyone can find a scraper. There are millions of them, probably a thousand in the Hill Country for each whole finished arrowhead. The Indians would start on one, hit a lick with a deer antler, chipping it, you see, and find out real soon that it wasn't going to work—too brittle, too soft—and toss it aside. So anyone can find a scraper. Still, I liked the old man. It wasn't his fault I couldn't find arrowheads.

Another thing I liked was Sputnik. This was when I was too young to really appreciate the raw beauty of the lure of the place, of the deer themselves, and was impressed instead more with little childlike things: old bleached antlers nailed up in the barn, the Spanish moss on the big oaks down on the creek, ball moss on the smaller scrub oaks up in the hills, and the terrifying way the rooster looked at me when I got out of the truck and tried to sneak across the yard and into Mr. Gold's cabin. No, secretly, I do think I loved it; you know how kids like to be scared. Sometimes I would sneak, creep around out of the rooster's view, pausing and peering out from behind little trees, rusty farm equipment, whatever, always working closer to the house, while other times I would catch a whiff of brazen growing-up-hood, Wildness, and would yell loudly and storm across the yard on a dead run, never noticing that I was frightening the rooster worse than he was me. Still, he was a rough-looking customer, and I remember him more than I do any brief, snatched glances of white-tails bounding into the cedars, in those early days anyway, on the spring trips. . . .

Sputnik only had three legs. The fourth was just not there; it was all withered and gone-looking. It had always been like that, but he was still the best deer dog in all of central Texas. There wasn't ever any competition or anything to prove this, but everyone said it was so, even other

ranchers who had pretty good deer dogs themselves, so it was true. At the age I was, of course, I liked Sputnik for the way he followed me around when I came to visit and for the way he lay in the dust and for the way he growled and sometimes ran interference for me when the big rooster tried to get too close and it was not until both Sputnik and Mr. Edgar Gold were gone and I was older that I learned that he had been the best deer dog in the county and that Mr. Edgar Gold had trained him, helped bring out and polish and guide this amazing talent he had for following and finding wounded deer. He was what they called a leopard dog.

My mother always called him "that ugly, spotted dog," and it was true, he did look like a hyena, but he was a smart dog—just fearful-looking, was all. He was my friend. I slept with him in the dust, I did, in the afternoons in the spring when we'd drive up there to check the place out. Leopard dogs always slept in the dust outside the porch; no one ever let a leopard dog into their house. They were too ugly. Most of them were sort of mustard-colored, with black spots and ovals. Blotches, my mother called them. I thought they looked pretty in the sunlight, when they moved, when they walked, when they bolted into a sprint of furred lightning to herd a chicken or a cow or get a goat or a goose back into formation. They were the fastest animal I'd ever seen, and fond of marshmallows. I brought Sputnik a sweating child's handful from Houston every time I came up there.

I imagine it will meet with opposition, when and if I ever do it, but I can double-guarantee you that if I ever have a child, boy or girl, if he or she wants one, he or she will have a leopard dog around the house for a pet. I will tell the wife, if she complains about the dog's ugliness, if she says it frightens the bridge players, this: that it is a good dog to have, even in the suburbs, because if one of the kids gets lost, a good Hill Country leopard dog can find it, even in the city. Mr. Edgar Gold's dog, I would tell her, could trail a deer all over central Texas.

But then again, maybe I'm fantasizing. I don't really think I'd keep such a noble dog as a Hill Country leopard dog penned up in the suburbs.

You don't ever forget things in the Texas Hill Country: old people you've met, dry creeks you've hiked, picnics you've had, leopard dogs you've known.

Mr. Edgar Gold is buried up on Sentinel Peak, in his family plot, where the wind always blows. You can see a long way up there; it's a nice view, a view he'd have liked. It's been ten years, but it won't ever seem longer. Things, like lives, take on significance in Texas deer hunting country, perhaps because they are lived so squarely and simply, and they are stronger and more basic than lives in the city, and they stand the eroding tests of time better. Things, memories included, last longer in Texas deer hunting country.

15
Godot

WE have a ringtail in camp. The thing supposedly keeps the snakes away, but mostly he just eats biscuits and gravy and sleeps all day. We never had problems with snakes before.

Yes, the ringtail is Cousin Randy's idea.

At night, he, the ringtail, not Cousin Randy, races around in the rafters of the bunkhouse and makes marvelous, daring, acrobatic leaps onto our sleeping bags, jumps which are, it seems, never executed until we have just drifted off into that vague halfway no-man's land that is not quite consciousness but not quite deep sleep, either. The kind of sleep you are in when the phone rings in the middle of the night and bleary-eyed you answer it and ask what time it is, only to discover that you have been asleep twenty minutes. It is the kind of sleep that reacts with something less than love when a furry creature from out of the night comes flying down from the rafters. The ringtail's name is Godot, but we call him lots of other things besides that. It should be pointed out real quick that not once in his short career has Godot ever been seen with a snake of any kind, live or dead, in his grasp. In fact, Godot will become airborne at the mere sight of a belt, a length of rope, a coil of jumper cables. But we never see any snakes around camp, so he is allowed to stay.

"He takes care of them at night," explained Cousin Randy. "And then he buries them over on the East Side—a long way off. That's why we never see any of them after he's finished them off," he said.

"I saw one hanging from a mesquite bush over on the back side of Buck Hill once," he lied. "It was a big one. It could have done a lot of damage." Cousin Randy looks out after Godot.

There are, however, some people in camp who are not fans of Godot.

Godot once climbed up on Grandaddy's leg as he was bringing a big buck into his sights. Another time he jumped up on the kitchen table and wolfed down Grandaddy's breakfast when his back was turned. Godot has even, on one sorrowful occasion, bitten Grandma Bass on the left earlobe. Grandaddy does not like Godot.

Godot is a slender animal with great wondering black movie-star eyes, and he is paradoxically as trusting as he is wily. He trusts everybody, even Grandaddy, and is sort of absent-minded, motoring about the cabin during the week that we are there each year under the singular impression that he is the sole reason we have arrived. Entertain me—you can see him thinking this. His eyes shine; he scampers, he capers, he knocks over the dominoes with his tail. We feed him tips and morsels, tidbits from our choice deer hunters' meals: thumb-sized bits of sirloin, a broad leaf of lettuce, a wedge of apple section, a square of brownie, a biscuit and honey. Grandaddy makes a special trip to the store before each hunt, makes a trip just for Godot, and buys a couple of lemons. Grandaddy tosses Godot little ringtail-sized bits of sour lemon and then laughs when Godot spits them out and rubs his paws across his whiskers, grimacing.

Once Godot threw up in Grandaddy's boots. Granted, he is a small animal, but still, it was not a pleasant thing to do. Grandaddy said he did it on purpose. Cousin Randy said he was just sick.

"Better there than on the floor, isn't it?" Cousin Randy cried.

"No," said Grandaddy. He had his tennis shoes on. It was a cold day, with a threat of snow or rain. Godot, of course, got better. Grandaddy predicted that he would really be sick if it happened again.

Godot was evidently quite attractive for a ringtail. We only saw him once a year, in the fall, really—never in the spring, when he was busy courting lady ringtails—but even in the fall, even as we were carrying ice boxes and lanterns in, sleeping bags and .270's, he would come barreling down the slope of boulder-studded Camp Hill, his legs reaching, drawing, folding under him in a quarter-horse's mad gallop, his long barred tail—as long as the entire length of his body, and then some—floating behind him, just trailing along oh-so-gently while the rest of him churned and

whirled like a wild thing in a hurry. And there would always be a group of lady ringtails following him. I don't
mean one or two, but a whole group: five, six. I think it was
his tail that did it. It was not hard to imagine him and his
little entourage lolling around in the shade, dozing, napping, licking their paws occasionally, waiting for night, only
to have their autumn dog-day siesta suddenly interrupted
by their leader's ears perking up at the sound of a truck
door being slammed and a screen door opened. I like to
picture him trotting over, cautiously, to a little rim-crest
look-out, hiding behind a cactus, maybe, like a bandit, and
peering down at the bunkhouse on the creek to make sure it
really was us, and then lickety-split, to his chippies' amaze-
ment, rushing straight down the hill.

That is why I think Godot was a bit of a romantic: the
way his lady friends followed him. Ringtails almost never
venture out in the daytime; they are strictly nocturnal. He
must have been quite the ringtail to cause them to bolt
inexplicably with him down the hill and towards the bunkhouse, or perhaps it was just that his excitement at seeing
us again was so infectious that they decided they wanted in
on some of whatever it was he was headed for, too. But
even Grandaddy, especially Grandaddy, laughed when
Godot's followers saw where he was headed: straight down
the hill for us and the camphouse, which was for the ringtails undoubtedly the Big City, the Heart of the Metropolis,
the Advent of Western Civilization. The alarm on their
faces was indescribable; the not-so-romantically attached of
them would instantly whirl and scoot back up the hill, running rabbit-style, ricochetlike, their small, clever minds
for once in a dither at the shock, while those more hesitant
to leave, for whatever reasons, would merely slam to a
stop, freeze, and then stamp and false-start back up the
hill, trotting a little ways up and then stopping each time,
looking first at Godot and then at us and then back down at

Godot, incredulous, before breaking into one final trot back up over the hill and behind the ridge, thinking, undoubtedly, "So sad, so sad when a mind snaps." At that distance, and by squinting your eyes, it was almost possible to believe you could actually see them shaking their heads. . . .

"Why a ringtail?" Grandaddy asked Randy once, at the domino table, after supper had been eaten and the dishes cleared. "Why not something useful, like a dog? But C. R. could only make his shy little half-smile, the way he always did when Grandaddy fumed because he couldn't understand something Randy did. Things like learning to play a harmonica and then a banjo and after that, a guitar, and then never doing anything with it, or bringing home a bird's nest with two tiny empty robin's-blue eggshells in it for his room, a grown man's room, after the nesting season was over, or working for free at Big Bend one summer, just to be out there, just room and board for a job doing the laundry at a series of cottages in the mornings. Cousin Randy'd just grin, as if he thought it was kind of neat that no matter how hard he tried—actually, he didn't really try at all, one way or the other—he'd made Grandaddy mad again.

One thing I regret that we no longer do in the new days as they did in the old days, and which is gone forever, and as such I will never experience, is hunting coons with lanterns and coonhounds in the middle of the night on the back side of the deer pasture, scrambling up rocks and crashing through dry cedar with a lantern in my hand and a little pack on my back with a couple of biscuits and sausages in it. Staying out all night, 'till first light, the way they, Grandaddy and Dad and Uncle Jimmy, used to do. Not worrying about anything.

Having a little campfire somewhere on the back side, under a big moon, when the dogs were just off down the creek or up in a meadow maybe, working but not finding. Sharing a canteen of water and one of those sausages and a biscuit or two. Maybe wearing a jacket or a windbreaker, if it was a quiet night with lots of stars out and November winter starting through. Listening to the dogs, Hondo and later Old Blue and later Sputnik, who was Old Blue's son and was born on the day the Russians launched the satellite, which made a big stir everywhere, even in Gillespie County. Watching the frost clouds come out of your mouth when you breathed, even through your nose. There was romance in it, and excitement, and a little danger, too, just enough to make your heart beat a little faster when you ran through the woods and the rocks under the big moon, and startled a sleeping animal that was obviously not a raccoon—cow? deer? One hoped so, because at night the woods were full of wild pigs, mean wild pigs, as well as cows and deer. It was a tradition, and a good one, and when you got back in at the crack of daylight, the sun coming up was gorgeous, as if by being up all night you had helped bring it in a little, as if it was just a little of your doing. And the coffee Uncle Jimmy made tasted good, as did the start of the new day, for when men are tired and exhausted together, they are either very irritable with each other or, paradoxically, closer, and for us it was never the irritable, but always the closer.

Dogs are good things to have in Texas deer hunting country. There aren't many people, and most everybody has a couple, sometimes three or four, so it is a real safe bet

to say that there are probably more dogs than people, at least in Gillespie County. And some of the dogs are as interesting as some of the people. Which is, heaven forbid, no reflection upon the people. Gillespie County just has some interesting dogs.

If you wanted to be a dog in Gillespie County, Texas, these are some of the skills that would be required:

You would need to be able to blood-trail wounded deer over slickrock, through creeks, up mountains, through cedar thickets, across meadows and pastures. You would need to do it well, for it is the worst of all imaginable things to wound a deer and cause it not to drop instantly but to run off in pain and linger and die somewhere up in a draw, confused and not understanding what it has done to deserve such pain, but it is an even blacker sin to do this to a deer and then not find it after it has run off and died or is still dying.

In Gillespie County, the better your dog, the better you are. This is a horrible thing to say, but I've noticed it too often; it's true. The responsible rancher's dogs are reflections of his training and discipline. It is surprising, the sort of surprise that makes you feel good, to discover that even the non-hunting ranchers usually own at least one good trailing dog, a dog that will find anyone's wounded deer, which is to me wonderful, for it matters not to the deer whose land he is dying on, nor does the rancher care as much about who shot the deer or on whose property as he does about stopping a wounded deer's suffering or trying to find a lost and just recently killed one. Lose a deer in Gillespie County, and if you go and knock on someone's farmhouse and ask to borrow their dogs, chances are they'll let you, and if they don't have any, they'll for sure know someone who does. The best strategy, of course, our strategy, is to spend an awful lot of time at the rifle range months beforehand—we owe it to the deer—and never to shoot at a moving deer. I understand that's not the way it's done in some places, but then we don't lose many deer, either. Not many at all. Got to brag, even: like four in forty-nine years. One per hunter's career. The system works.

If you were a dog in Gillespie County, you would also need to be able to cut cattle, herd sheep, guard chickens and keep company: be pleasant, wag tail, laugh at jokes, droop eyes at trouble. Mope on days when the bills came. Not chase the mailman like a city dog. Avoid getting snakebitten. Stay away from bobcats.

Also, you might be called upon to do this: hunt coons.

It is the one reason most dogs in Texas deer hunting country can bear the dry, dusty, depressingly hot summers: the thought of fall and of sleeping all day in the cool sunshine, and then running all night, doing what they have been bred to do, doing what is in them. Running coons. In summer there is no wind and their throats parch, and they lie down in the dust and stare straight ahead, not seeing anything, but actually they are seeing something, and it is five months away and is cool with frost in the air and dark blue sky at night and stars like jewels and sometimes night thunder without rain, and it is what they live for, it is inside them. And though some of them do not do it, because their masters do not let them do it, or because they are not in shape for it, or because they are too old, it is nonetheless still inside them, this hunting, in the fall. You can make them not do it, but you cannot make it not be inside them.

16
Ringtails and Raccoons

THE trouble with being a ringtail in Gillespie County is that it is almost like being a raccoon. The dogs that hunt the coons at night can sense there's a little difference, in the way ringtails won't head for water, but instead for the rocks, but the dogs don't care, and for that matter, neither do the fur buyers, not too much, anyway, because although raccoon skins are more valuable, the buyers will still take a ringtail skin if you bring it in. So people go coon hunting, not ringtail hunting, but if the dogs cross a ringtail's path, the ringtail had better run. It doesn't seem fair. I have always wondered if ringtails dislike raccoons for this.

It's the one time, the one thing in camp we refuse to pamper Grandaddy on. He discovered the place, he's hunted it for forty-nine-years—he's the founding father, he's been here every year, even when they camped in a canvas tent with a dirt floor in the winter, and he's paid a lifetime of dues and seen a lifetime of sights and now deserves a little downhill coast, a little pampering, so we sort of cater to him in his choice of hunting spots, and cook his meals for him, and help him clean his deer when it is really cold and his hands are shaking—but we do not go coon hunting as he used to do when he was young and could run all day and all night and loved just being out under the night sky with Howard's and Mr. Edgar Gold's dogs. He sulks, crosses his arms, looks down at his feet, disgusted, and you can tell what he's thinking, and he's livid, because we're his own grandchildren, he truly doesn't understand

it, but it's Dad and Uncle Jimmy, too. They used to go on coon hunts and stay up all night, and it was fun, and they'd catch a coon every now and then, or a ringtail, and it was the men and the dogs, but they have done it and now they do not. It is one of those things that is over with. Some things have to end; perhaps Godot, and not hunting coons, will become Cousin Randy's and my tradition, as hunting them with Sputnik and Old Blue was Grandaddy's. He scowls, sits at the domino table, and looks puzzled and worried when he thinks about it.

17
Autumn

GRANDADDY is sick. He is tough, but not well at all. He has had one stroke this spring and his hands cannot close with strength. He will probably not be able to come to the deer pasture this fall. A photo album, with pictures from the deer pasture, lies on his coffee table by the ashtray, by the television gizmo. It makes me sad to think of him laughing when he was twenty-three and down at the deer pasture, and how I never knew him then and wish I had.

I love him; yes, that is the right word for it.

Grandaddy is not so well. My children, if I ever have any, will never get to hunt the deer pasture with him.

None of us will ever hunt the deer pasture with him again.

What made him turn in on Howard's ranch road that hot and dusty summer day forty-nine years ago? What made him stop there? What made him not sleep late that morning and not head off into the Hill Country, searching for a place to hunt? What made him take all the right left turns at the right times, and all the right right turns?

It's the secret of life itself, I'll bet. I've got the next fifty years to puzzle over it.

SEP 19 2014